Theoretical Perspectives of Strategic Followership

The concept of followership, like leadership, is not new to the extent that it has been around since the beginning of creation. It is so pervasive in human interactions that attempts to study it are often met with ridicule. In the organization literature, followership, a complementary role to leadership, was often ignored until recently when scholars observed that followers have as much a role to play in the leader–follower relationship. *Theoretical Perspectives of Strategic Followership* focuses on one type of followership—strategic—which is an emergent phenomenon. Similar to leadership, followership has been defined as a role, process, and capacity. Indeed, others consider it as socially constructed. In addition to the definitions, the relatively sparse literature has identified antecedents, outcomes, and moderators of followership.

The book combines both the macro (strategic management) and micro (psychological) foundations of strategic followership to encourage research not only among strategic management scholars but also those in the micro fields of organizational behavior, human resources management, and industrial psychology.

Dr. David Baniyelme Zoogah is Associate Professor at Xavier University, Cincinnati, Ohio, USA.

Routledge Studies in Leadership Research

CSR, Sustainability, and Leadership
Edited by Gabriel Eweje and Ralph J Bathurst

Revitalising Leadership
Putting Theory and Practice into Context
Suze Wilson, Stephen Cummings, Brad Jackson, and Sarah, Proctor-Thomson

Women, Religion and Leadership
Female Saints as Unexpected Leaders
Edited by Barbara Denison

"Leadership Matters?"
Finding Voice, Connection and Meaning in the 21st Century
Edited by Chris Mabey and David Knights

Innovation in Environmental Leadership
Critical Perspectives
Edited by Benjamin W. Redekop, Deborah Rigling Gallagher, and Rian Satterwhite

After Leadership
Edited by Brigid Carroll, Suze Wilson, and Josh Firth

Creative Leadership
Contexts and Propsects
Edited by Charalampos Mainemelis, Olga Epitropaki, and Ronit Kark

Theoretical Perspectives of Strategic Followership
David Baniyelme Zoogah

For more information about the series, please visit: www.routledge.com/New-Directions-in-the-Philosophy-of-Education/book-series/NDPE

Theoretical Perspectives of Strategic Followership

David Baniyelme Zoogah

NEW YORK AND LONDON

First published 2019
by Routledge
52 Vanderbilt Avenue, New York, NY 10017

and by Routledge
2 Park Square, Milton Park, Abingdon, Oxon, OX14 4RN

Routledge is an imprint of the Taylor & Francis Group, an informa business

© 2019 Taylor & Francis

The right of David Baniyelme Zoogah to be identified as author
of this work has been asserted by him in accordance with
sections 77 and 78 of the Copyright, Designs and Patents Act
1988.

All rights reserved. No part of this book may be reprinted
or reproduced or utilised in any form or by any electronic,
mechanical, or other means, now known or hereafter invented,
including photocopying and recording, or in any information
storage or retrieval system, without permission in writing from
the publishers.

Trademark notice: Product or corporate names may be
trademarks or registered trademarks, and are used only for
identification and explanation without intent to infringe.

Library of Congress Cataloging-in-Publication Data
A catalog record for this title has been requested

ISBN: 978-1-138-67986-3 (hbk)
ISBN: 978-1-315-56352-7 (ebk)

Typeset in Sabon
by Apex CoVantage, LLC

My Dad, Kpelingatba, and his grandchildren, Coniah Alahada Zoogah and Jalen Baniyelme Cloud Zoogah.

Contents

	Acknowledgments	viii
	Preface	ix
1	Introduction	1
2	Strategic Role	13
3	Strategic Situations	39
4	Strategic Decisions and Actions	67
5	Strategic Interactions	88
6	Strategic Outcomes	118
	Index	128

Acknowledgments

I am grateful to all those who nurtured the growth of strategic followership, particularly all those who contributed or participated in the symposia and learning conferences on strategic followership at the Academy of Management Annual Meetings between 2015 and 2018. Their input shaped my understanding of strategic followership. Standing out in this group is Dr. Erica Anthony, Morgan State University. We organized the Professional Development Workshops, Symposia, and Teaching and Learning Conference sessions at the Academy of Management (AOM) annual meetings together. Thank you very much. I also owe a lot of gratitude to Aleshia Zoogah, Peter Bycio, Robert and Margaret Cloud, Mike Peng, Oded Shenkar, Raymond Noe, Richard Zoogah, Evelyn Larbi, Jim Walsh, Stella Nkomo, and all other friends who in indescribable ways supported this project. To all I say, THANK YOU!

Preface

As bad leadership manifests in greater proportion, followership is being recognized as important in not only organizations but also society. Scientific studies similar to those in leadership are likely to assist in undoing the harm caused by bad leadership. Given the central role of theory in science, theoretical perspectives that facilitate the study of followership in organizations seems indispensable. That is the purpose of this book. I discuss perspectives that can be used to investigate questions on strategic followership. The followership role which can be enacted by individuals and organizations centers on strategic value. By examining theories with strategic import, we discern the strategic role of followers. As a result, I introduce the concept of strategic role which is discussed with role context, role activity, role process, and role dynamics. I discuss theoretical perspectives related to the environment, resources, transactions, and outcomes which correspond to strategic situations, strategic decisions and actions, strategic interactions, and strategic value respectively.

My goal in writing this book is twofold. First, I build on the first book where I introduced strategic followership. I believe followers can contribute meaningfully to organizations' strategic goals in much the same way that leaders do. Second, I am interested in facilitating the study of strategic followership which is aided by the availability of theoretical perspectives. That is why I emphasize the approaches—emergent, a bottom-up process involving individual actors, and interactive, a lateral process involving organizational actors. I organize the book into six chapters.

1 Introduction

What are the various ways by which one can study strategic followership? This question raises two fundamental issues: methodological approaches and theoretical perspectives. This book is about the latter. A book that provides a theoretical lens equips those curious about the phenomena but lack the instruments for studying it. I write this book knowing full well three major facts. First, strategic followership is new, and there is a lack of empirical evidence on the concept and phenomena. In order to nurture its growth, there have to be ways of studying it. Theoretical lenses for studying it are therefore significant. Second, there is a divide between micro and macro scholars. The consolation, however, is that there is also growing interest in narrowing the divide as evidenced by the micro-foundations of strategy (Foss & Lindenberg, 2013) and the macro-foundations of organizational behavior (Ployhart, 2015), human resources management (Becker & Huselid, 1998), and industrial organizational psychology (Ployhart, 2012; Zoogah, 2012).

Third, the perspective of strategic followership may be considered either naivety or revolutionary. Those who view it as naivety should pause and reflect on the trumping of leadership at the national level in America. They would admit, if they are honest with themselves, that strategic followership is necessary. There are supervisors like that in organizations as evidenced by the abusive supervision literature (Tepper, 2000, 2007). Kellerman (2004, 2008) calls that bad leadership. Strategic followership demands more of followers in bad leadership situations. It could also be interpreted as revolutionary because of the call for followers to 'challenge' not only themselves but also leaders who are acting in ways that diminish value. In other words, followers are called on to rise to their better selves. The Op-Ed in the New York Times on Sept 5, 2018 which detailed the resistance within the White House is an illustration of restorative followership, a dimension of strategic followership. The author indicates that "we believe our first duty is to this country, and the president continues to act in a manner that is detrimental to the health of our republic."[1] The good thing is there is a growing need across the spectrum—business, politics, and society for individuals who are willing to contribute *more* to organizations, nations, and society, respectively.

2 Introduction

The relationship between leaders and followers is like a network where supervisors are subordinates to their superiors and the latter, in turn, are subordinates to their supervisors (Uhl-Bien, Riggio, Lowe, & Carsten, 2014). More concretely, operatives are followers to supervisors who, in turn, are followers to managers who, in turn, are followers to executives. The latter are followers to the members of the board of directors. The growing need to contribute to organizations thus encompasses all organizational members (Collinson, 2006). Given the emerging focus on followership as a significant factor in leadership dynamics, it is important to empirically investigate followership to the same degree as leadership in organizations (Yukl, 2012). It is unfortunate that few studies have paid attention to followership (Uhl-Bien et al., 2014). Of the limited followership studies, two perspectives have gained prominence. One perspective focuses on operative behaviors in the relational interface, such as compliance of followers to leaders. According to this view, followers (e.g., subordinates) enact their roles in ways that enhance or diminish leadership and organizational outcomes. Another perspective focuses on the social constructive behavior of followers (DeRue & Ashford, 2010). It posits that through relational interactions, followers co-produce relationships, behaviors, and identities with leaders (Fairhurst & Grant, 2010; Shamir, 2007) that enable the relationship to achieve its goals (Uhl-Bien et al., 2014). Both perspectives suggest that followers seek to contribute value (e.g., legitimacy, sales, capabilities, knowledge, and resources) to their organizations (Zoogah, 2014).

Since the global recession, there has been heightened practitioner interest in the contributions and value followers create within organizations in their work roles (Knights & McCabe, 2015). Additionally, practitioners seek to examine the response of these followers when they perceive the attenuation of value within their organizations. For instance, why did Cynthia Cooper and Sherron Watkins express concern about value-diminishing activities in WorldCom and Enron, respectively? Cynthia Cooper exposed WorldCom's mismanagement of funds when she informed its board that the company had covered up US$3.8 billion in losses through phony bookkeeping. Sherron Watkins expressed similar concerns to Kenneth Lay, the CEO, about the financial schemes of Enron that eventually took down the company (Swartz & Watkins, 2003; Watkins, 2003). These subordinates are generally considered to be whistle-blowers (Dungan, Waytz, & Young, 2015). The followership literature considers them as responsible followers (Alford, 2008) and strategic followers (Zoogah, 2014). They were concerned about the diminishing value of their organizations. Consequently, they not only halted the diminishing value created by the bad leaders but also took steps to restore the lost value.

This leads us to a key question: How do followers contribute value to organizations? A review of the literature suggests three major perspectives. The first perspective focuses on the contextual factors of bad leadership, such as, but not limited to, incompetence, unethicality, and abusive supervision. This perspective suggests that through restorative behaviors (actions that restore any diminished value) followers can contribute value to organizations. Followers who restore any diminished value as a result of bad leadership behaviors affect reputational, image, and relational organizational values and, consequently, contribute to the strategic objectives of their organization. Studies show that legitimacy, a major outcome of organizations, depends on reputational, image, and relational values (Wilkin, Campbell, & Moore, 2013). Cynthia Cooper and Sherron Watkins typify restorative followers. They engaged in restorative behaviors that benefited their companies (Zoogah, 2011). By exposing WorldCom's mismanagement of funds, Cynthia Cooper's actions forestalled future organizational losses (Near & Miceli, 2016).

The second perspective suggests that followers also contribute value to organizations in good leadership contexts because not all followers function in bad leadership contexts. Although value in good leadership contexts is not diminished, a follower may perceive that it can be magnified. Striving to generate superior value in the context of good leadership is also a form of strategic followership. Studies of this perspective are sparse. Zoogah (2014) defines this perspective as transcendent followership, the process by which a follower strives to achieve optimal value or extraordinary outcomes despite challenges or constraints. Similarly, Pina e Cunha, Rego, Clegg, and Neves (2013) define a transcendent follower as "someone who expresses competence in terms of their management of relations with self, others and organization" (p. 87). Their definition focuses on the competence of followers and assumes the enactment of behaviors, some of which may not be strategic. In contrast, Zoogah (2014) views competence as a driver of followers' strategic behavior. Followers who are competent can generate superior value for organizations in good leadership contexts. Both contend that additional research on transcendent followership is warranted.

The third perspective suggests that followers contribute value to organizations when they enact roles that maintain the status quo or social order. In the follower–leader interface, maintenance behaviors, such as endorsement, harmonizing, hedging, and imitation, enable the relationship to operate normally (Zoogah, 2014). The environmental context, which is defined by normalcy, represents a state of balance. Followers in that operative mode expect to maintain the state of order. With regard to value creation, the value is neutral; there is neither a decrease nor an increase in value. From a behavioral perspective, the normalcy state represents task performance, which would normally be expected of the follower who is required to work toward maintaining that state. Research extends this notion by suggesting that leaders often imitate the actions of followers to maintain the status quo when experiencing certain competitive social pressures (Ross & Sharapov, 2015).

The three perspectives—restorative, maintenance, and transcendent—represent a psychological approach to strategic followership. It is a bottom-up approach that suggests that followers as individuals contribute

4 Introduction

value to organizations through restorative, maintenance, and transcendent behaviors. In other words, it is *interpersonal strategic followership*.

The second approach, which I term interactive, is lateral. It focuses on organizations as entities. Embedded in the dominant strategic management paradigms—industrial-based view (Porter, 1985), resource-based view (Barney, 1991), and the institution-based view (Peng, Sun, Pinkham, & Chen, 2009) is the idea of leadership and followership. Organizations that have a competitive advantage are leaders in the industry and their behaviors, activities, and strategies influence other organizations to follow them. Strategic leadership enables organizations to achieve and maintain strategic competitiveness in the 21st century (Ireland & Hitt, 1999). Research on strategic leadership has grown speedily across the social sciences and resulted in a profusion of knowledge on the meaning, dimensions, contingencies, and system of strategic leadership. Finkelstein, Hambrick, and Cannella (2009) observe that "hundreds of academic and applied articles, books, and monographs on top executives and their organizations have been written" (p. 8) in the past thirty years.

In contrast, there seems to be virtually little on strategic followership of not only subordinates (Uhl-Bien et al., 2014) but also organizations (Zoogah, 2014). With regard to organizations, Ross and Sharapov (2015) examine when leading firms *follow* using competitive dynamics. They argue that leaders can avoid dethronement by imitating the actions of followers. Specifically, they note that:

> imitation can be an effective means of staying ahead, even in the absence of mimetic social pressures . . . because the leader's imitation of follower actions represents equilibrating moves to maintain the status quo in reaction to the disequilibrating actions that the follower undertakes to catch up with the leader.
>
> (p. 658)

Fuller, Akinwande, and Sodini (2003) examine how Taiwanese companies lead and follow foreign technology organizations in innovation. They identify three categories of companies—those that lead, those that follow, and those that do neither—in the electronics industry of Taiwan.

The literature on strategic leadership shows that in organizations' attempt to achieve competitive advantage, they undertake activities, some of which include influencing other organizations to either yield or facilitate those outcomes (for a detailed review of that literature, see Finkelstein et al., 2009). For example, organizations sometimes deliberately choose to follow other organizations for strategic purposes. Matthews and Cho (2001) find that latecomer firms are not "late entrants"; rather, the latecomer firms' market entry is a "matter of strategic choice" because they "are very well established and well-endowed firms which delay entry until technological and market trends are clear—and then move in with superior forces to take the lion's share of the market." They contend that it is a rational "followership" strategy, a matter of strategic choice. The buyer–supplier literature also suggests that suppliers sometimes learn the processes of buyer firms for imitative purposes or because of strategic coercion (Fuller et al., 2003; Heide & John, 1990; Han, Wilson, & Dant, 1993). How then do organizations engage in followership, and how do those roles contribute to their short-term and long-term outcomes?

Drawing from the interorganizational relationships literature (Oliver, 1992) which shows that organizations relate with each other as peers or equals, it can be argued that organizations sometimes assume followership roles in relating with other organizations assuming leadership roles. The 'following firm' may submit to the influence of the 'leading firm' implicitly or explicitly (Ross & Sharapov, 2015). That type of followership is considered *interorganizational strategic followership*. The relationship may be positional (i.e., one organization adopts a particular position relative to another) (Matthews & Cho, 2001).

Both interpersonal and interorganizational approaches are based on a number of assumptions. First, I assume that both the leader and the follower are equal in terms of value creation (EQUALITY). Theoretically, either party can contribute as much value as possible. It is not based on the ability to contribute value but the status or power. It contrasts with the traditional view of leadership where the follower is subordinated to the leader and can only take actions that yield value if and only if permitted to do so. Second, I assume the leader, by authority vesting, is open to the contribution of the follower (READINESS). Even though the authority vested in leaders is for the sake of accountability, it is often used as a basis to assert power. To the extent that the leader is not open to the contributions of the follower, it is likely the latter may be unsuccessful in restorative and transcendent actions. The third assumption is that the follower does not seek to subvert the leader (PURITY OF INTENTIONS). Strategic followers are other-oriented. As a result, their actions are not directly for self gain. It does not mean that they cannot be recognized by the leaders or organizations. That recognition is important in that it will motivate future strategic behaviors. It might also motivate other followers to enact strategic followership behaviors. The purity of intentions allays the leader's fears about the actions of the follower. The last assumption is that whatever constraints are encountered by the follower are surmountable (i.e., FLATNESS). To the extent that constraints can be overcome, followers are likely to enact strategic behaviors. Given these assumptions, I offer the following propositions:

1. The strategic objectives of an organization depend on the value created by (a) its members in their respective roles or (b) itself as a following firm (STRATEGIC OBJECTIVES).

6   *Introduction*

2. Followers create value when they relate with leaders in a way that generates strategic outcomes (a) indirectly (i.e., through emergence processes) or (b) directly (i.e., through interactional processes) (RELATIONSHIP).
3. The relationship depends on the strategic situation with the leader (STRATEGIC SITUATION).

> 3a. In good situations where the leader generates ordinary or subpar value, the follower strives to generate extraordinary or superior value. The greater the value enhancement, the more transcendent the follower (VALUE ENHANCEMENT).
> 3b. In bad situations where the leader diminishes value, the follower strives to restore the diminished value. The greater the value restoration, the more restorative the follower (VALUE RESTORATION).

4. The resultant value curve is concave for restorative value but convex for transcendent value such that followers will weight restorative action more than transcendent action ($V_r > V_t$; VALUE CURVE).

Testing these propositions and disproving the assumptions requires theoretical lenses. That is the purpose of this book. I suggest theories (macro and micro) that have strategic import and can therefore be used to study strategic followership. In addition to drawing from the strategic management literature to suggest relevant theories, I review the psychology and organizational behavior literature for theories that are similar to those at the macro level. For example, agency theory (Jensen & Meckling, 1976) is a macro (organizational level) theory, but it has psychological equivalence in agencies of the self (Markus & Hamedani, 2007). The theories I suggest are neither exhaustive nor exclusive. So, I encourage additional theories that can enhance our understanding of strategic followership.

In sum, followership generally is characterized by the relational environment, relational transactions, relational resources, and relational outcomes. These characteristics also apply to strategic followership. Strategic management theories that relate to environment (e.g., institutions), transactions (e.g., agency), resources (e.g., information asymmetry), and outcomes (e.g., performance) can therefore be leveraged to study strategic followership. These theories are discussed in Chapters 1 through 5. The theories are structured as follows. First, I discuss the *background* of strategic followership in the introductory chapter. Second, I discuss STRATEGIC ROLE THEORY and its relationship to strategic followership. Role theory has been studied in diverse disciplines—sociology, psychology, and organizations. However, in the organizations and management domains, the focus has principally been in leadership (i.e., leaders and followers) because of the dominant psychological focus. I review

Introduction 7

role theory as it relates to followership to show the gap and conclude by highlighting the need for a strategic role perspective. I use role theory to explicate strategic role theory. Specifically, I clarify the different meanings of strategic followership to show how individuals and organizations acting in the followership role (as in leadership) can contribute value directly and indirectly (Sy, 2010). I situate strategic role theory within the broader role theory. It is generally agreed among leadership scholars that followership, like leadership, is a role (Uhl-Bien et al., 2014). I outline the various ways the strategic role perspective has been viewed in other disciplines. My purpose for doing so is to distinguish operative followership that is evident in the extant paltry literature from strategic followership, which is emergent. Included in this chapter is an elaboration of how strategic followership fits with the strategic role perspective. In doing so, I show how the various perspectives of strategic role relate to the two major components of strategic followership—restorative and transcendent. The linkage is likely to enable researchers to explore either component separately or to integrate them.

Third, I discuss STRATEGIC SITUATIONS, the environment of strategic followership. I term theories that focus on the environment of strategic followership *meso theoretical lenses* because the environment that comprises internal and external relational contexts is influenced by phenomena at the micro and macro levels. I focus on strategic situations and strategic dynamics. Not only do the behaviors and cognitive orientations of leaders and followers change, but the structure and progression of the relationship also change. Given the centrality of dynamics in relational exchanges, it seems important to discuss theoretical lenses for studying strategic dynamics. The leadership literature shows situations as one major determinant of the leader–follower exchange. Recently, there has been a distinction between psychological and strategic situations. The latter are proposed as major determinants of strategic followership (see Zoogah, 2014). Studies of strategic followership therefore require an understanding of the theoretical lens that will facilitate understanding of strategic situations and their dynamics. Strategy theories that focus on the environment include institutions, network, routines, symbolism, and culture.

Fourth, I focus on theories that are appropriate for STRATEGIC DECISIONS AND ACTIONS of followers. Effective decisions and actions are based on the availability of resources, tangible and intangible. As a result, resource-based theories are discussed. They include competence, information asymmetry, resource dependence, and psychological capital. Included are crisis decision-making theory and strategic response theories, prospect theory of decision-making, and game theory.

I follow this discussion with theories that seem suitable for STRATEGIC INTERACTIONS involving followers and leaders. Agency, exchange

8 *Introduction*

(social and economic), political, tournament, signaling, and shared mental models are discussed along with strategic trust. Strategic interactions center on the orientations (particularly calculative) of followers to interrelate with leaders in the accomplishment of some tasks or achievement of some goals. When leaders socialize with followers out of a desire to influence the response of the latter toward an outcome, the interaction is strategic. Theoretical perspectives for understanding such interactions include symbolism theory and political theory. Symbolism theory, which is similar to signaling theory, indicates that the followers may interact with leaders merely to, but not really intending to, show impactful responses. Political theory refers to the study of concepts and principles that individuals and groups use to describe, explain, and evaluate political events and institutions. It focuses on issues of representation, justice, equality, and rights. Strategic cognition theories, such as mental models, are mechanisms that followers can use to manipulate the behavioral responses of leaders. The cognitive representations or scripts of followers are likely to orient the leaders toward fundamental outcomes of individual, group, and organizational. Further, follower–leader exchanges involve affective processes that determine relational and organizational outcomes. I briefly discuss theoretical lenses that examine the affective reactions of followers toward individual and organizational strategic objectives. Two theories are strategic trust and social exchange.

I conclude the book by discussing strategic value and levels of strategic followership. Value theory encompasses a range of approaches for understanding how, why, and to what degree people value things and whether the object of valuing is a person, idea, object, or anything else. Thus, value theory focuses on concepts and principles underlying value attribute by individuals, groups, and organizations. Value is viewed from subjective and objective lenses and across several dimensions—psychological, economic, political, financial, and relational. Strategic followership proposes a value curve in which some followers act to restore value when bad leaders destroy it and others act to advance value when good leaders' actions limit relational and tangible value to organizations. One might therefore ask why is social value orientation (SVO) which centers on values, not included. SVO is like a game where a person's preference about how to allocate resources (e.g., money) between the self and another person. It corresponds to how much weight a person attaches to the welfare of others in relation to their own. In that regard, it can be used to study follower–leader exchanges. However, because participants are asked to imagine they will *neither* meet *nor* interact with the other and they do not receive feedback about the choices of the other person, strategic considerations are removed from their choices (Balliet, Parks, & Joireman, 2009). As a result, SVO does not have strategic implications; it merely focuses on the motives of the actors in a social interaction. It is for that reason that it is not included as a theoretical lens in this chapter. Given the significance of level theory and the increasing intersection of the micro-foundations and macro-foundations perspectives, it is important to clarify the levels of analysis of strategic followership.

In sum, the theories in this book are intended to encourage empirical research. They should facilitate empirical investigation of the model in Figure 1.1.

As a multiple mediated model, it depicts the process by which strategic followership manifests. Factors within the external and internal environments influence the transaction interface involving the follower and the leader. In that interface, the occurrence of strategic situations (e.g., unethical behavior) result in strategic role activation (e.g., moral duty) that, in turn, triggers strategic affect (e.g., trust). That affect also drives followers to make strategic decisions (e.g., plans) to take some strategic action that

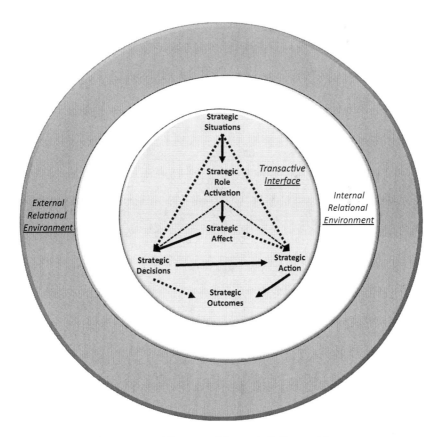

Figure 1.1 Environment and Process of Strategic Followership

10 *Introduction*

ultimately results in some strategic outcomes. This process is shown by the bold arrows. The broken arrows are direct effects which theoretically are inconsistent with the theory. For example, the emergence of a strategic situation does not immediately lead to strategic decisions or actions. Rather, they activate the strategic role of the follower. Nevertheless, they can be examined for falsification purposes.

Through such research additional theories might emerge that will be included in future updates. Of course, these are my views of theories that seem suitable.

Note

1. https://www.nytimes.com/2018/09/05/opinion/trump-white-house-anonymous-resistance.html

References

Alford, C. (2008). Whistleblowing as responsible followership. In Riggio, R., Chaleff, I., & Lipman-Blument, J. (Eds.), *The Art of Followership: How Great Followers Create Great Leaders and Organizations* (pp. 237–251). San Francisco, CA: Jossey-Bass.

Balliet, D., Parks, C., & Joireman, J. (2009). Social value orientation and cooperation in social dilemmas: A meta-analysis. *Group Processes & Intergroup Relations*, 12(4), 533–547.

Barney, J. (1991). Firm resources and sustained competitive advantage. *Journal of Management*, 17(1), 99–120.

Becker, B. E., & Huselid, M. A. (1998). High performance work systems and firm performance: A synthesis of research and managerial implications. In *Research in Personnel and Human Resource Management*, 16, 53–101.

Collinson, D. (2006). Rethinking followership: A post-structuralist analysis of follower identities. *The Leadership Quarterly*, 17(2), 179–189.

DeRue, D. S., & Ashford, S. J. (2010). Who will lead and who will follow? A social process of leadership identity construction in organizations. *Academy of Management Review*, 35(4), 627–647.

Dungan, J., Waytz, A., & Young, L. (2015). The psychology of whistleblowing. *Current Opinion in Psychology*, 6, 129–133.

Cunha, M. P., Rego, A., Clegg, S., & Neves, P. (2013). The case for transcendent followership. *Leadership*, 9(1), 87–106.

Fairhurst, G. T., & Grant, D. (2010). The social construction of leadership: A sailing guide. *Management Communication Quarterly*, 24(2), 171–210.

Finkelstein, S., Hambrick, D. C., & Cannella, A. A. (2009). *Strategic Leadership: Theory and Research on Executives, Top Management Teams, and Boards.* Strategic Management. Oxford: Oxford University Press.

Foss N. J., & Lindenberg, S. M. (2013). Microfoundations for strategy: A goal-framing perspective on the drivers of value creation. *Academy of Management Perspectives*, 27(2), 85–102.

Fuller, D., Akinwande, A., & Sodini, C. (2003). Leading, following or cooked goose? Innovation successes and failures in Taiwan's electronics industry. *Industry and Innovation*, 10(2), 179–196.

Heide, J. B., & John, G. (1990). Alliances in industrial purchasing: The determinants of joint action in buyer-supplier relationships. *Journal of Marketing Research*, 24–36.

Ireland, R. D., & Hitt, M. A. (1999). Achieving and maintaining strategic competitiveness in the 21st century: The role of strategic leadership. *Academy of Management Perspectives*, 13(1), 43–57.

Jensen, M. C., & Meckling, W. H. (1976). Theory of the firm: Managerial behavior, agency costs and ownership structure. *Journal of Financial Economics*, 3(4), 305–360.

Kellerman, B. (2004). *Bad Leadership: What It Is, How It Happens, Why It Matters*. Boston: Harvard Business School Press.

Kellerman, B. (2008). *Followership: How Followers Are Creating Change and Changing Leaders*. Boston: Harvard Business School Press.

Knights, D., & McCabe, D. (2015). Masters of the Universe: Demystifying leadership in the context of the 2008 global financial crisis. *British Journal of Management*, 26(2), 197–210.

Markus, H. R., & Hamedani, M. G. (2007). Sociocultural psychology. In Kitayama, S., & Cohen, D. (Eds.), *Handbook of Cultural Psychology* (pp. 3–39). New York: Guildford.

Matthews, J. A., & Cho, D. S. (2001). Combinative capabilities and organizational learning in latecomer firms: The case of the Korean semiconductor industry. *Journal of World Business*, 33(4), 139–156.

Near, J. P., & Miceli, M. P. (2016). After the wrongdoing: What managers should know about whistleblowing. *Business Horizons*, 59(1), 105–114.

Oliver, C. (1992). The antecedents of deinstitutionalization. *Organization Studies*, 13(4), 563–588.

Peng, M. W., Sun, S. L., Pinkham, B., & Chen, H. (2009). The institution-based view as a third leg for a strategy tripod. *Academy of Management Perspectives*, 23(3), 63–81.

Ployhart, R. E. (2012). The psychology of competitive advantage: An adjacent possibility. *Industrial and Organizational Psychology*, 5(1), 62–81.

Ployhart, R. E. (2015). Strategic organizational behavior (strobe): The missing voice in the strategic human capital conversation. *The Academy of Management Perspectives*, 29(3), 342–356.

Porter, M. 1985. *Competitive Advantage*. New York: Free Press.

Ross, J. M., & Sharapov, D. (2015). When the leader follows: Avoiding dethronement through imitation. *Academy of Management Journal*, 58(3), 658–679.

Shamir, B. (2007). From passive recipients to active co-producers: Followers' roles in the leadership process. Follower-centered perspectives on leadership: A tribute to the memory of James R. *Meindl*, 9–39.

Swartz, M., & Watkins, S. (2003). *Power Failure: The Inside Story of the Collapse of Enron*. New York: Doubleday.

Sy, T. (2010). What do you think of followers? Examining the content, structure, and consequences of implicit followership theories. *Organizational Behavior and Human Decision Processes*, 113(2), 73–84.

Tepper, B. J. (2000). Consequences of abusive supervision. *Academy of Management Journal*, 43(2), 178–190.

Tepper, B. J. (2007). Abusive supervision in work organizations: Review, synthesis, and research agenda. *Journal of Management*, 33(3), 261–289.

12 *Introduction*

Uhl-Bien, M., Riggio, R. E., Lowe, K. B., & Carsten, M. K. (2014). Followership theory: A review and research agenda. *The Leadership Quarterly*, 25(1), 83–104.

Watkins, S. (2003). Former Enron vice president Sherron Watkins on the Enron collapse. *Academy of Management Perspectives*, 17(4), 119–125.

Wilkin, C. L., Campbell, J., & Moore, S. (2013). Creating value through governing IT deployment in a public/private-sector inter-organisational context: A human agency perspective. *European Journal of Information Systems*, 22(5), 498–511.

Yukl, G. (2012). Effective leadership behavior: What we know and what questions need more attention. *Academy of Management Perspectives*, 26(4), 66–85.

Zoogah, D. B. (2011). A multilevel model of virtuous followership for leader—Follower relationship effectiveness. Presented at Society for Industrial and Organizational Psychology Conference in Chicago, IL.

Zoogah, D. B. (2012). A cooperative advantage: An alternative informed by institutional theory. *Industrial and Organizational Psychology*, 5(1), 116–119.

Zoogah, D. B. (2014). *Strategic Followership: How Followers Impact Organizational Effectiveness*. New York, NY: Palgrave Macmillan.

2   Strategic Role

What role does followership play in fulfilling the strategic objectives of organizations? This question is best answered by considering what a role is, and its strategic context. Role theory has been studied in diverse disciplines—sociology, psychology, and organizations. However, in the organizations and management domain, the focus has principally been in leadership (i.e., leaders and followers) due to the psychological focus. I extend role theory to explicate strategic role theory and elaborate on how strategic followership fits with the strategic role perspective. Specifically, I discuss how the various perspectives of strategic role relate to the two major components of strategic followership—restorative and transcendent.

2.1 Followership as a Role

Scholars of leadership and the nascent subdomain of followership generally agree that followership is a role (Uhl-Bien, Riggio, Lowe, & Carsten, 2014; Kelley, 1992). But what is a role and what is followership? A review of the literature shows diverse definitions of followership. While some define it as a state—"the acceptance of influence from another person or persons without feeling coerced and toward what is perceived to be a common purpose" (Stech, 2008: 48), others define it as process—"followership is the process people use to follow" (Rost, 2008: 54), and still others define it as "the capacity or willingness to follow a leader" (Uken, 2008: 139). Zoogah (2014) defines it as "the role enactment process" (p. 6), consistent with followership as role-enactment (Heller & Van Til, 1982), and Hollander's (1974) definition of a role as "a set of behaviors which are appropriate for a position which an individual fills" (p. 19).

Role theory has been studied in diverse disciplines—sociology, psychology, and organizations. As Johns Heine (quoted by Biddle, 1979: 1) indicates, "the importance of role theory is undeniable, its range of influence has been vast, research engendered in its name diverse and bountiful . . ." Biddle (1979: 4) defines role theory as "a science concerned

14 *Strategic Role*

with the study of behaviors that are characteristic of persons within contexts and with various processes that presumably produce, explain, or are affected by those behaviors." A review of the voluminous role theory literature shows a number of characteristics that can be summarized as (1) patterned behaviors associated with (2) social positions that are (3) governed by expectations and (4) embodied with consequences, to which individuals (5) are socialized. Even though these characteristics emerge from psychological research on individuals, the interorganizational literature suggests that they may apply to organizations.

Organizations are structured hierarchically. As a result, there have been role-based views of followership in the context of hierarchical roles. These studies are interested in how followers work with leaders to achieve organizational outcomes. Organizations generally seek to determine the proper mix of follower characteristics and behaviors that promote desired outcomes (Graen & Uhl-Bien, 1995). In their review of the followership literature, Uhl-Bien et al. (2014) discuss a number of ways by which role theory has been applied to followership. A review of the literature shows a number of conceptual and empirical works that identify different types of followers. First, based on the characteristics of individuals in followership roles, Zaleznik (1965) identified four types of followers—impulsive, compulsive, masochistic, and withdrawn—as a function of the dominance–submission and activity–passivity dimensions. Second, with a focus on role effectiveness, Kelly (1988) proposed effective followers as "courageous, honest, and credible" (144). Using the degree of dependence (dependent vs. independent) and activity (passive vs. active) he identified five types of followers—alienated, exemplary, conformist, passive, and pragmatist. The latter are in the center, midway on the two dimensions. He advocates for exemplary followers, arguing that the "the best followers are anything but passive sheep—they are actively engaged and exhibit courageous conscience (Kelley, 1992)" (Uhl-Bien et al., 2014: 90).

Third, Chaleff (1995) focuses on the expected response to follower roles by proposing courageous followership styles—implementer, partner, individualist, and resource—based on the degree of support from, and challenge to, the leader (Chaleff, 1995, 2003, 2008). His foundational premise is that "leaders rarely use their power wisely or effectively over long periods unless they are supported by followers who have the stature to help them do so" (Chaleff, 2003: 1). A fourth typology is proposed by Lipman-Blumen (2005), who is interested in the relationship with toxic leaders; she discusses why followers so willingly obey toxic leaders and suggests three categories of followers some of which actually enable and support bad leaders. The first type, "benign followers," are gullible and go along unquestioningly with what a toxic leader is saying, primarily for pragmatic reasons, such as keeping their jobs. The second type, "the leader's entourage," serves as the toxic leader's alter ego. They

Strategic Role 15

do this by committing to the leader's agenda. The third type, "malevolent followers," are driven by greed, envy, or competitiveness and work against the leader.

Howell and Mendez (2008) focus on followers' orientation toward their roles. They propose three types of follower role orientations—interactive, independent, and shifting. The interactive role supports and complements the leadership role. As Uhl-Bien et al. (2014) indicate, the "interactive role orientation can be a highly effective and dedicated follower, a relatively ineffective (Kelley's 'sheep') follower, or even part of a toxic leader's loyal entourage" (p. 91). The independent role orientation involves high levels of autonomy and, in a positive vein, high levels of competence that complements the leader's role. Exemplars of this role include high-level professionals, such as engineers, physicians, university professors who work independently but contribute to the organization's goals. In the shifting-role orientation, a follower alternates between the leader and the follower role depending on the circumstances.

Others—Carsten and colleagues (Carsten, Uhl-Bien, & Jaywickrema, 2013; Carsten, Uhl-Bien, West, Patera, & McGregor, 2010)—examine "how followers describe their beliefs regarding the ways they view and enact their roles, as well as the personal qualities and contextual characteristics they see as facilitating or impeding their ability to be successful as a follower" (Uhl-Bien et al., 2014: 92). They identify different passive and proactive follower schema. The former see their role as being obedient and deferent (e.g., "sheep"; Kelley, 1992) while the latter view their roles as partnering with leaders by taking ownership and accountability for achieving organizational objectives (e.g., active co-contributors, Chaleff, 1995; Kellerman, 2008; Shamir, 2007). In that regard, their typology is not novel; it is merely a reformulation of Kelley (1988), Chaleff (1995), and Kellerman (2008).

Unlike the preceding typologies that have primarily been within the management domain, Kellerman's (2008) typology is from a political science domain. Based on the level of engagement, she categorizes followers as isolate, bystander, participant, activist, and diehard. While isolates are completely detached and bystanders observe but do not participate, participants are in some way engaged. Activists feel strongly about their leaders and act accordingly while diehards are deeply committed and prepared to die for their causes. Motivated by a desire to engage followers to act as agents of change, Kellerman argues that "followers have more power and influence than they are traditionally accredited" (Uhl-Bien et al., 2014: 91).

Building from insight into implicit leadership theories (ILTs) which proposes that leaders have tacit knowledge about their attributes and behaviors (Offermann, Kennedy, & Wirtz, 1994), Sy (2010) proposed that followers also have knowledge about the traits and behaviors that define them. He identified prototypes, composed of industry, enthusiasm, and

16   *Strategic Role*

good citizenship attributes, and antiprototype. composed of conformity, insubordination, and incompetence attributes. The consequences of these prototypes include interpersonal outcomes of relationship quality, liking, trust, and satisfaction, as well as high performance expectations, liking, and Leader-Member Exchange (LMX) (Epitropaki, Sy, Martin, Tram, & Topakas, 2013). Leaders' implicit theories of followers and followers' implicit theories of followers interact to influence relationship quality and follower performance (Sy, 2011).

In addition to traits and behaviors, followers sometimes perceive their role as shaping leaders' actions. Dvir and Shamir (2003), as well as Howell and Shamir (2005) and Shamir (2007), show that the principal role of followers is in influencing the leader and facilitating the emergence of leadership (Uhl-Bien et al., 2014). Given the "important role of followers in defining and shaping the latitude of leader's action" (Hollander, 1993: 29), Dvir and Shamir (2003) examined the relationship between followers' developmental characteristics and followers' ability and tendency to actively contribute to the emergence of transformational leadership. They found that while followers' initial developmental level (e.g., self-actualization needs, collectivist orientation, critical-independent approach, active engagement in the task, self-efficacy) relates positively to transformational leadership among indirect followers, they relate negatively to direct followers. Howell and Shamir (2005) propose a conceptual framework that presents followers as having a more active role than that assumed in traditional leadership research. Consistent with Chaleff's (1995) contention that powerful leaders need to be counteracted by powerful followers, Howell and Shamir (2005) show that followers have to recognize and play more active roles in avoiding the pitfalls and abuses of power associated with charismatic leadership, for example.

In addition to the characteristics of roles, behavior is emphasized by role theory (Biddle, 1979). Followership researchers have also focused on the kinds of behaviors individuals enact as part of their follower roles. The degree to which followers engage in their roles is highlighted by Kelley (1992, 1988). Zaleznik (1965) and Kelley (1988) propose resistance and proactive behaviors as a result of the shift from production economies to knowledge economies. Proactive behaviors focus on the creative and deliberate ways that employees plan and act on to influence, change, and alter their environment in ways they deem fit. Proactive behaviors include influence tactics (Kipnis, Schmidt, & Wilkinson, 1980), feedback-seeking (Ashford & Cummings, 1985), taking-charge behavior (Morrison & Phelps, 1999), prosocial rule-breaking (Morrison, 2006), voice (Morrison & Milliken, 2000; Van Dyne & LePine, 1998) influencing work structures (Parker, Wall, & Jackson, 1997), personal-initiative taking (Parker, Williams, & Turner, 2006), and championing (Andersson & Bateman, 2000). Grant and Ashford (2008) integrate these perspectives to define proactive behavior as "anticipatory action that employees take to impact themselves and/or their environments" (p. 8). They characterize it as applicable in "any set of actions through anticipating, planning, and striving to have an impact" (p. 9). Proactive behavior is also relevant in both in-role and extra-role activities. Proactive behaviors are widely examined in the social sciences, but followership researchers seem most interested in how employees relate to leaders and how leaders receive and respond to followers' proactive behaviors (Whiting, Maynes, Podsakoff, & Podsakoff, 2012). This interest emerges because research seems to indicate that leaders are not always open to the proactivity of followers (Grant, Parker, & Collins, 2009; Whiting et al., 2012); leaders see proactivity as insubordination, a threat (Frese & Fay, 2001), an ingratiation attempt (Bolino, 1999) or overstepping bounds. Carsten and Uhl-Bien (2012) found that followers with high co-production beliefs reported greater voice and constructive resistance. In addition, they found co-production beliefs interact with contextual factors, such as considerate leader style, overall relationship quality, and autonomous work climate for voice, but not for constructive resistance. Different effects were observed for voice behaviors.

Followers tend to also be obedient and subordinated because of the belief that leaders are responsible for making decisions, solving problems, gathering information, and setting goals (De Cremer & Van Dijk, 2005). These behaviors fit with the authority view of organizational hierarchies where leaders or supervisors are seen as 'authority figures' who are more capable and effective than others (Weber, 1968) and followers are perceived as executors of orders (Heckscher, 1994). Obedient behaviors of followers have been confirmed in laboratory (Burger, 2009; Hoption, Christie, & Barling, 2012) and cross-sectional (Blass, 2009; Carsten & Uhl-Bien, 2013) studies. Indeed, Van Vugt and colleagues (King, Johnson, & Van Vugt, 2009; Van Vugt, Hogan, & Kaiser, 2008) theorize that the tendency to follow is part of natural selection. In other words, there are some individuals who naturally act as followers and voluntarily subordinate themselves to others.

However, research since the beginning of the 21st century has begun to question the obedience view because of the contention that not all 'followers' follow. Studies show that followers enact resistance behaviors (Tepper, Duffy, & Shaw, 2001; Tepper, Duffy, Henle, & Lambert, 2006) particularly in the contexts of abusive supervision or unethical leadership. Tepper et al. (2001), for example, found that constructive resistance that involves well-intended efforts to open a dialog with the supervisor (e.g., ask for clarification or negotiate) and dysfunctional resistance which involves passive-aggressive responses in which subordinates might act as if they are too busy to complete the request, pretend they did not hear it, or say they forgot to manifest in abusive supervision.

In a follow-up study Tepper et al. (2006) investigated managers' reactions to subordinate resistance. They found that managers viewed

18 *Strategic Role*

subordinate resistance differently. They were more receptive to the negotiation of resistance—uniformly dysfunctional (all manifestations of resistance are bad) or multifunctional (some manifestations of resistance are more functional than others)—only when it was from high-LMX subordinates.

Other behaviors include followers' willingness to carry out orders or doing as leaders instruct them (Carsten et al., 2010). These latter acts are termed maintenance behaviors because they maintain the relationship or status quo (Zoogah, 2014). Considering that order, harmony, adherence to standards, and regularity are valuable outcomes for organizations (Cameron & Whetten, 1983), maintenance behaviors contribute value to organizations. Maintenance behaviors that sustain the relationship or programs of leaders contribute maintenance value (see also Zoogah, 2014).

2.2 Strategic Role

Fundamental to strategic followership is the term *strategy*. Considering that followership is a role, it seems important to differentiate role as in operative followership from strategic role as in strategic followership. According to the *Oxford English Dictionary*, the term *strategy* refers to a "behavior or sequence of behaviors elicited in response to a particular stimulus or situation," "an action plan," "course of action" or "a course of implementation."[1] Etymologically, it is often traced to Greek origins where it meant 'strategos' or 'strategia,' which means 'a general.' The plan, scheme, or trick for surprising or deceiving an enemy is a stratagem. In business, a stratagem refers to "any artifice, ruse, or trick devised or used to attain a goal or to gain an advantage over an adversary or competitor."[2] However, Horwath (2006) suggests that the first treatises that discuss strategy are from the Chinese during the period of 400 to 200 BCE, one of which is Sun Tzu's *The Art of War*, written in 400 BCE, which is a major work on military strategy. In military parlance, the term *strategic* is associated with long-range aircraft and missiles. In other words, the strategic role of the aircraft and missiles is to enable the military to achieve its fundamental (war) outcomes—victory over the enemy.

Even though business strategy derives from military strategy (Chandler, 1962; Keller, 2008), it has developed into a discipline with its own concepts. Chandler (1962) defines strategy as "the determination of the basic long-term goals and objectives of the enterprise and the adoption of courses of action and the allocation of resources necessary for carrying out these goals." Strategy thus focuses on identification of *ends* and the *means* to achieve those ends. The ends can be categorized as short term or long term, and the means include tangible and intangible resources (Mintzberg, 1998). It connotes two meanings—*ends* achieved via stratagem or subterfuge (Path A), and ends achieved via genuine resources

Strategic Role 19

(Path B). A follower who says, "I have a strategy to outwit him," in response to a request by a leader to support an unethical action operates via Path A while a follower who indicates that "she has achieved her strategic objective" in response to a question about her outcomes is following Path B. Functionally, Path A is mediated by the stratagems of strategic followers but unmediated in Path B.

Based on role as a behavior that is characteristic of a person in context, the functions of a role (Biddle, 1979), and a review of the strategy literature I identify a number of strategic roles and their characteristics. I also propose mechanisms by which the strategic roles lead to specific outcomes. Collectively, they point toward strategic role theory that fits with strategic followership. Role behaviors are "contextually bound" and functional (Biddle, 1979: 6). It is therefore important to explain the functions and contexts of strategic roles. By context I mean the physical or psychological features that provide meaning to the specific descriptors that elucidate the strategic roles. Strategic followership roles are congruent with some contexts. In strategic alliances, a subordinate from a partner organization merely represents his or her organization in the alliance exchange that compels him or her to interact with the 'team leader' (i.e., supervisor), who is from the focal organization. The strategic role he or she plays is embedded in the alliance context (Zoogah, 2006).

2.2.1 Strategic Role Context

There is a context for roles (Biddle, 1979). The characteristics that regulate behavior enable the actors to achieve certain outcomes. Without those regulatory attributes, organizations, for example, may not be able to function effectively within that particular context. By effectively I mean operating in a way that yields positive outcomes for the organization as well as members of the institution. The International Organization for Standardization (ISO), which provides regulatory mechanisms for relating with the environment (i.e., ISO 14000), for example, specifies normative standards that organizations follow to be consistent with environmental sustainability. These normative standards align the actions of a 'following' firm and those of the 'leading' firm. Furthermore, to the extent that the ISO influences the behavior of organizations vis-à-vis pro-environmental behavior, the ISO can be considered a leader and organizations as followers. Both enact their respective roles consistent with the norms of the institution (Scott, 2014). In that regard, institutional theory, particularly the more positive area of positive institutional work that emphasizes "the creation or maintenance of institutional patterns that express mutually constitutive experiential and social goods" (Nilsson, 2015: 370) is not only for individuals in positions of influence but also for the targets of positivity. For that perspective, theories that explicate role-based cognitions, affect, and behaviors define a context for the

20 Strategic Role

particular roles. Thus, both micro and macro theories function as contexts for roles. In the case of macro theories that derive from strategic management, the contexts are role-based (i.e., strategic roles).

2.2.2 Approaches to Strategic Role Contexts

Fundamental to strategic followership is the notion that a follower contributes value that enhances the strategic outcomes of any or all of the following entities: follower, leader, department, and organization. These multilevel attributes suggest two major approaches to the study of strategic followership: intraorganizational and interorganizational. The intraorganizational approach focuses on the hierarchical (top-down) relationships between supervisors and subordinates. In other words, it follows the micro–macro relational structure within organizations. Typically, studies adopting this approach focus on how individual followers' strategic behaviors contribute to the strategic advantages of organizations. It involves emergence processes where the cognitive, affective, and behavioral orientations of individual followers emerge at the organizational level to affect strategic outcomes of organizations. In that regard, the approach might be termed the psychological perspective of strategic followership. Psychological theories related to cognition, affect, and behavior of followers are deployed to explain how the strategic behavior of followers contribute to the organizations' strategic outcomes.

In contrast, the interorganizational approach focuses on the lateral relationships between organizations in followership roles. In that regard, it centers on organization-to-organization interactions. Because the focus is at the organizational level, it can be regarded as the business policy perspective. Strategic management theories that indicate strategic roles enacted by macro units or organizations are used. In their study, *When The Leader Follows: Avoiding Dethronement Through Imitation*, Jan-Michael Ross and Dmitry Sharapov (2015) ask the question, "When is imitation of follower actions an effective competitive strategy for a leader?" They then use a competitive dynamics perspective and institutional theory reasoning—"imitation can be an effective means of staying ahead, even in the absence of mimetic social pressures"—to argue that "the leader's imitation of follower actions represents equilibrating moves to maintain the status quo in reaction to the disequilibrating actions that the follower undertakes to catch up with the leader" that result in what they term "action imitation" and "positioning imitation" strategies that are "moderated by the degree of environmental uncertainty, by the extent of the leader's initial advantage, and by the difference between leader and follower capabilities" (p. 658). They discuss "endogenous and exogenous contingencies of *competitive interactions*" and advance "competitive dynamics as a predictive theory of performance outcomes"

(p. 658). This might be considered the business policy perspective. It might also be considered the interactive perspective because the organizations interact with each other as equals. Both the psychological and business policy perspectives explain strategic roles. A strategic role is therefore defined as a unique characteristic that proffers a distinct fundamental advantage.

In sum, an understanding of strategic followership requires consideration of four major elements: environment, transaction, resources, and outcomes. The environment influences the transactions between the follower and the leader in much the same way that the resources (tangible and intangible) shape those transactions. The outcomes, in turn, depend on these three elements. Strategic theories that relate to the environment, transactions, resources, and outcomes may shed light on the phenomenon of strategic followership.

2.3 Typology of Strategic Role Theories

The strategic role contexts suggest that some theories seem more suitable than others in explaining strategic followership roles. Some strategic roles contexts focus on the relational environment of strategic followership. They include culture, routines, institutions, and symbolism, which focus on the values, patterned activities, regulatory mechanisms, and representative symbols that underlie the context of strategic followership. Strategic situations emerge from these elements. Consequently, they enable the study of strategic situations as discussed in Chapter 3. Other strategic role contexts focus on the transaction between the leader and the follower. Bad and good leadership situations emerge from the transactions between actors. Thus, the theories may help explain how the transactions trigger, enable, shape, or constrain strategic followership. These transaction-based theories include transaction cost exchange, agency, political, tournament, signaling, and game theories.

The third category of strategic role contexts center on the resources, broadly defined, that influence the transactions and outcomes. Social exchanges generally require resources. The resources may be tangible or intangible. Micro (e.g., psychological capital) and macro (resources dependence) theories can thus help explain how resources influence not only the transactions but also the outcomes of strategic followership. Resource-based view, information asymmetry, resource dependence, psychological capital, and competence are theories in this category. Last, some strategic role contexts focus on the outcomes of strategic followership. Transactions yield outcomes for constituents in the relational interface. Thus, outcome-based theories explain either the nature of the outcomes or why those particular outcomes are achieved by the constituents. They include stakeholder and performance theories.

22 Strategic Role

Table 2.1 Strategic Role Contexts and Theoretical Lens in Strategic Followership Dimensions

Theoretical Lens	Strategic Role		Strategic Followership Framework	
	Role Context	Example	Restorative	Transcendent
Resource-based	Resource	Financier		X
Resource dependence	Deprivation	Borrower		X
Institutional theory	Norm	Regulator	X	
Information (asymmetry) theory	Knowledge	Informants (police)		X
Agency theory	Agency	Director		X
Exchange theory	Transaction	Buyer/Friend		X
Political theory	Constituency	Representative	X	
Performance theory	Behavior	Reporter		X
Network theory	Network	Boundary-spanner	X	
Stakeholder theory	Stake	Investor	X	
Routine theory	Routine	Recruiter	X	
Signaling theory	Signal	Supporter	X	
Symbolism theory	Symbol	Chief	X	
Culture theory	Value	Priest/Pastor		X
Tournament theory	Gamer	Competitor		X
Power	Office	President		X

2.4 Strategic Role and Strategic Followership Dimensions

Earlier, I mentioned various macro theories that implicitly focus on followers. However, the question that remains is how the various theoretical perspectives relate to the two major components of strategic followership framework—restorative and transcendent. Such a linkage is useful in enabling researchers to explore either component separately or integratively. Table 2.1 shows the theoretical lenses that relate to the dimensions of strategic followership. First, I focus on theories that might be applied to transcendent followership.

2.4.1 Strategic Role and Transcendent Followership

One characteristic of significance in transcendent behavior is overcoming personal or environmental challenges (Bateman & Porath, 2003). To the extent that a theoretical lens is embedded with challenge, it seems likely to be applicable to transcendent behavior. Studies employing that theory are encouraged to show the degree to which the follower surpassed challenges. Resource dependence theory, which proposes that a person or an organization that relies on another person or organization is beholden to that individual or entity, suggests that the entity in need of resources is deprived. A follower who is dependent on a leader for resources (e.g., expertise) would have to overcome the challenge of deprivation to interact with the leader in a way that yields extraordinary outcomes. The leader may not be open to goodwill of the follower. That lack of openness may limit the success of the follower's initiative. At the firm level, the credibility of the following firm that lacks expertise is likely to be questioned by the leading firm.

Agency theory focuses on the representation of the principal by the agent. The transcendence of the agent can be studied. Tourish (2014) argues that organisational actors who do not occupy formal leadership roles can make a contribution. To what extent does the agent yield his or her self-interest to that of the principal? Even though the agent is contractually bound to the principal the degree to which he or she exceeds the expectations of the principal by surpassing personal challenges can be a source of insight for strategic followership.

The theory of power, which has been studied extensively, tends to focus on the leader. However, it can be applied to strategic followership not in the sense of malevolence (i.e., a follower seeking to overthrow a leader) but of benevolence (a follower leveraging power to achieve extraordinary outcomes). The follower has to overcome the challenge of the authority structure. It is generally recognized that bureaucracy is a constraint not only to speed to market but also decision-making. A strategic follower therefore has to overcome what might be perceived as insubordination. Social network theory, which proposes that the relations of individuals are a web of resources that can be accessed, relates to strategic followership. The social network of a follower can be leveraged not only to overcome challenges (e.g., spanning) but also to achieve superior outcomes.

Culture within organizations refers to anything more than an ideology cultivated by management for the purpose of control and legitimation of activity (Smircich, 1983). A general and more popular definition is a complex set of values, beliefs, assumptions, and symbols that define the way in which a firm conducts its business. Culture has pervasive effects on an organization. An organization's culture defines who its relevant employees, customers, suppliers, and competitors are and how it will interact with these key actors (Louis, 1983). As a result, Barney (1986) suggests that organizational culture can be a source of sustained competitive advantage. Three conditions for culture to be a source of sustained competitive advantage include value (it must enable the organization to do things and behave in ways that enhance sales, lower costs, improve margins, or in other ways add financial value to the firm), rarity attributes that are not common to a large number of other organizations, and imperfectly imitable (cannot be copied by other firms).

24 Strategic Role

As representatives of shareholders, managers or supervisors enforce the culture of the organization. As a result, the value associated with culture may be suboptimal. It thus provides an opportunity for transcendent followers to optimize the subpar value. A strategic follower might proffer ideas on control and legitimation of activities either within or external to the organization. A follower could offer ideas on how traditional production or operational practices might be improved with better practices. The strategic followership perspective—achievement of superior outcomes as a function of corporate culture—differs from the operational perspective of followership where individuals adhere to the rules and values of organizations to maintain the status quo. Bligh (2011) asks, "What is the role of organizational culture and structures in suppressing or fostering a climate for effective followership?" When culture fosters a climate for effective followership, it enables followers (interpersonal context) to create value (Uhl-Bien et al., 2014). However, strategic followership asks, 'How can followers leverage organizational culture to generate extraordinary outcomes?' This question centers not only on generating value but also on capturing value in excess of what would ordinarily be created.

Information asymmetry is a situation where one party to a transaction has more information than the other party (Akerlof, 1970; Rothschild & Stiglitz, 1976, 1978; Moro, Fink, & Maresch, 2015). In strategic followership, it could be the leader or follower. However, given bureaucratic structures of organizations supervisors tend to have more information than subordinates. However, the bases of power theory (French and Raven, 1959) suggests that to the extent that followers have expertise, they are likely to have information that places them at an advantage. In this era of knowledge revolution, which empowers or advantages individuals who are curious, creative, or analytical (Shapiro, 1999), followers may gain information that leaders may lack. The access to information may thus enable subordinates to enact the strategic followership role. As I indicated earlier, the role context is knowledge where a follower could be an informant. The informant proffers information that may be more valuable and therefore yield greater outcomes. Such information may enable the immediate supervisor of the follower to make decisions that have strategic value. At the organizational level (i.e., the interactive perspective), a following firm might use such information to generate superior outcomes.

The social dimension of exchange—social exchange theory—has been examined extensively in the micro field. Lacking is the economic dimension of exchange—economic exchange theory. This is unfortunate because the essential element of the latter theory, which centers on governance of transactions (albeit economic) has social relevance. That relevance occurs because of relational contracting. As Williamson (1979) indicates, "the pressures to sustain ongoing relations takes on the properties of

Strategic Role 25

'a minisociety with a vast array of norms beyond those centered on the exchange and its immediate processes' " (p. 238). A follower and a leader engage in a relational contract such that the reference point for effecting adaptations is the "entire relation as it has developed . . . [through] time" (p. 238). The role context is the relational contract where as a collaborator or partner or friend, the follower is bound by the norms of the relational contract throughout the entire period.

The specifications of the relational contract can involve a follower as a basis for either performance of his or her role or the transcendent intervention. With regard to the latter, governance mechanisms—vertical integration, outsourcing, and mixed governance—that are often used for market contracts can be applied to relational contracts. Vertical integration is equivalent to the follower engaging in the transcendent activities all by him- or herself while outsourcing refers to passing the responsibility of managing the improvement of the sub-optimality to someone else who may have expertise or resources (e.g., time) with the expectation that the value-generated benefits the constituents in the relational interface. As discussed below, governance is also possible in restorative followership. For example, a follower may request a peer of the bad leader to use his or her social competence to restore any value diminished by the leader. Mixed governance occurs when the follower collaborates (Rost, 2008) or partners with another person to restore any value diminished by the leader.

Tournament theory in the management literature has been employed to help explain compensation structures (e.g., Messersmith, Guthrie, Ji, & Lee, 2011), and other rank-order contests (Boudreau, Lacetera, & Lakhani, 2011). Tournament theory is generally attributed to Lazear and Rosen (1981) for the original formulation, but Rosen (1986) added extensions. According to these authors, a tournament is a contest in which actors compete for a prize that is awarded based on relative rank and is designed to incent an optimal level of effort (Connelly, Tihanyi, Crook, & Gangloff, 2014). Tournaments can be designed strategically when firms set up the mechanisms such that choosing optimal prize spreads maximizes the productive output of the tournament.

This idea of strategically designing the tournament is explored in a unique way by Seip and Grøn (2016). They identify leaders and followers in repeated games by analyzing an experimental, repeated (50 rounds) game where the row player shifts the payoff between small and large values—a type of "investor" and the column player determines who gets the payoff—a type of "manager." They find that (a) the investor (row) most often is a leading player and the manager (column) a follower; (b) the game has an efficient cooperative strategy where the players alternate in receiving a high payoff, but the players never identify, or accept, that strategy; and (3) if the information used by the players is closely associated with the leader–follower sequence and that information is

26 Strategic Role

available before the player's decisions are made, the players switched leader–follower strategy, primarily, as a function of information on the leader's investment and moves and, second, as a function of the follower's payoff. The authors found that it is always the manager (i.e., follower) that "achieves the largest payoff" (p. 1). This finding suggests that followers achieve greater outcomes or create more value. Furthermore, the literature suggests that second-movers (i.e., followers) best respond to the first-movers' (i.e., leaders) choices. Shogren and Baik (1992) investigate the form of exogenous leadership that arise in sequential contests—the case of the "favorite leader" versus "underdog follower." Their experiments identified several key behavioral departures. In that contest, the favorite leader tends to submit effort levels that are no different from the favorite's expenditures in the simultaneous move game. In their role as followers, underdogs sometimes seek to balance or counter the likelihood of winning across players rather than maximizing their expected payoff (Dechenaux, Kovenock, & Sheremeta, 2015).

Given tournament theory's assertion that the main purpose for paying a CEO high pay is not to provide incentives to that person him- or herself but instead to motivate the rest of the top managers to work super hard so they can win the tournament to become the next CEO, followers can be induced to create strategic value not with the intention of succeeding the leader but to mobilize the capabilities and potentials of the followers to improve suboptimal value. Like governance tournaments may also apply to restorative followership. They can harness to drive of followers to restore diminished value. The idea of spreads—(the difference between post- and pre-restoration values)—can be applied to transcendent (and restorative) followership tournament. If the value spread is minimal, followers are unlikely to be motivated to 'compete' to enhance subpar value (and to restore diminished value) restore so that the total value of the tournament drops. However, a value spread that is large may be detrimental because it induces so much effort that followers might be overwhelmed, which can reduce the efficiency of the transcendent tournament. Thus, optimal transcendent tournaments can be designed such that transcendent value is highest when optimal value spreads maximize strategic outcomes of the tournament to relational constituents.

2.4.2. Strategic Role and Restorative Followership

Next, I turn to theories that might be applied to restorative followership. Organizational routines, "repeated patterns of behavior that are bound by rules and customs and that do not change very much from one iteration to another," promote continuous change (Feldman, 2000: 611). In examining latecomer firms as strategic initiatives, Matthews and Cho (2000) suggests that latecomer firms' knowledge consists of the "routines and methods learned and that are integrated through the exercise of its combinative capabilities need to assemble disparate items process technology and bring them to a high level of coherence and performance in mass production" (p. 145). Organizational routines theory suggests firm-level strategic followership that focuses on restorative value: remedying the mistakes of leading firms by restoring the value of the industry to a higher level. In addition, the plethora of fields of institutions and disciplinary foci has resulted in diverse definitions of institutions. Williamson (2000), for example, considers institutions as the ensemble of deeply embedded norms and values, constitutions, legal and regulatory frameworks, policies, governance, and negotiated agreements that are 'institutionalized' in various structures, networks, value chains, and so on. North (1990) considers them simply as the "rules of the game" and distinguishes formal institutions—laws, regulations, and their supporting apparatuses (enforcement agencies, regulatory bodies, etc.)—from informal institutions—norms, values, and beliefs that define socially acceptable behavior. The role context—norms—suggests that a follower is likely to contribute superior value in the role of a regulator or enforcer. The strategic follower role can be enacted formally or informally. Research could thus examine how a strategic follower as a regulator or enforcer functions either disparately or comparatively. The theory is helpful in explaining how institutions contribute to the effective restoration of value diminished by bad leadership behavior.

Stakeholder theory predicts that organizations that take into consideration the interests of constituents with a stake in their business are likely to be effective (Pfeffer, 1998). The level of dependence indicates how organizations relate with the stakeholders (Frooman, 1999). Primary stakeholders, those that are directly affected by the activities of organizations, differ from secondary stakeholders, who are indirectly affected. Leaders, departments, organizations and other relational constituents are stakeholders of strategic followers. As a result, the latter have to differentiate primary stakeholders (e.g., leaders and organizations) from secondary stakeholders. Studies examining the process by which followers differentiate their stakeholders and the degree of dependence of followers on stakeholders and vice versa will be interesting. Schneider (2002) tried to develop a theory of stakeholder leadership following Bass and Steidlmeier's (1999: 200) suggestion of discussing "leadership in the context of contemporary stakeholder theory." Caldwell, Karri, and Vollmar (2006) suggest that "organizational governance can profitably be viewed from the ethical perspective of organizational followers—employees of the organization to whom important ethical duties are also owed" (p. 207). Furthermore, Pless and Maak (2011) build on Maak and Pless' (2006) assertion that "building and cultivating ethically sound relations toward different stakeholders is an important responsibility of leaders in an interconnected stakeholder society" (p. 101) to suggest that "followers become stakeholders of the leadership project" (p. 6). Caldwell et al. (2006) "propose that the followers' perspective about the ethical duties of organizational governance provides insight about how organizations

28   Strategic Role

can improve their bottom line performance, create greater wealth for stakeholders, and contribute to a better society" (p. 208). It suggests that followers have a duty to restore value diminished as a consequence of the unethical behavior of leaders. The value could be for either primary or secondary stakeholders. Leveraging psychological contract principals, the follower can add to the principal's short-term wealth (Golembiewski, 2000) by redefining role performance as a responsibility or duty.

Signaling theory ascribes costs to information acquisition that resolve information asymmetries between leaders and followers. Followers do not always have accurate information about the value optimization of the leader; the behavior of the latter signals the quality of value optimization and reduces information asymmetries. While bad behaviors are presumably reliability signals of value destruction because such behaviors will not withstand the rigors of moral rectitude or ethics tests, good behavior may be a means by which leaders communicate otherwise unexpressed interested in superior value. I draw from Kirmani and Rao (2000) to illustrate how strategic followers may receive signals from two leaders: good and bad. Although the leaders know their own value potential (how capable they are in creating or destroying value), followers do not, so information asymmetry is present. Consequently, each leader may or may not signal his/her true value creation potential to followers. When good leaders signal, they receive what might be termed Payoff A, and when they do not signal they receive Payoff B. In contrast, bad leaders may receive Payoff C when they signal and Payoff D when they do not signal. Signaling thus represents a viable strategy for good leaders when A > B and when C > D. Given these circumstances, good leaders are motivated to signal and bad leaders are not, which results in a separating equilibrium. In such cases, followers may be able to accurately distinguish between good and bad leaders. In contrast, when both types of leaders benefit from signaling (i.e., A > B and C > D), a pooling equilibrium results, and followers are not able to distinguish between the two types of leaders. The same reasoning applies to followers. Leaders may lack knowledge about their potential to create value (e.g., function effectively as partners or collaborators). Consequently, they have to rely on the signals from followers about their ability to contribute to the strategic objectives of the constituents in the relational interface. There may be payoffs (i.e., benefits) to the signals. For example, the signals may lessen the resistance of leaders to the contribution of followers.

Signaling theory is therefore a lens to investigate the strategic value of followership. Signals from both leaders and followers could be examined either within a particular period or longitudinally. The signals could also be looked at comparatively to determine the efficacy or quality of the signals. For example, are signals of leaders and followers in the public sector different from those in the private sector, and what factors will account for the signal differences? Furthermore, research on signals in good and bad leadership contexts could be compared to see which ones are stronger. The noise in good leadership contexts might be low, making signal detection weak, whereas that in bad leadership context might be high, which could elevate signal detection. Other studies may focus on the optimal balance among accuracy, informativeness, and transparency (i.e., signaling value) in both contexts. Such studies might examine moderations as exemplified by Janney and Folta (2006).

Related to signaling, a corollary, costly signaling theory, which explains how individuals use risky behaviors to spread partially hidden information about their positive qualities (e.g., intelligence—Millet & Dewitte, 2007) or social dominance (Neiman, 1998), may also be applied to strategic followership. According to costly signaling theory, the positive behaviors of followers may be viewed as self-advertising strategy, a follower's way of positioning him- or herself for access to resources during unforeseen future times of need (Boone, 1998). A costly signal from a social perspective is one whose reliability is ensured because it has greater costs due to the efficacy requirements; the signal may be costly to produce or have costly consequences. According to the theory, altruistic actions are "social signals," indicating the society about the sender's personal qualities. Costly signaling, such as providing benefits to others, helps solve the problem of maintaining cooperation in a group (Gintis, Smith, & Bowles, 2001). Why will followers invest time and energy in signaling to leaders? The logic of costly signaling theory suggests that the restorative behavior of followers toward leaders will occur only if the leaders who observe the signal will respond with high probability in ways favorable to the follower.

Symbolism, the use of symbols to represent ideas or qualities, often involves interpreting the meanings of the symbols (i.e., symbolic interaction). Organizational symbolism, which conjures up a wide variety of meanings within the organizational community, refers to the study of a particular action, object, or language that conveys a meaning that may be abstract. As a result, it refers to the study of the expressive functions of organizational life (Ornstein, 1986). It relates to strategic followership through symbolic capital, the "credit of renown," associated with prestige and social relations of followers either in the eyes of the leader or other constituents in the relational interface. Bourdieu (1997) indicates that the highest profits in symbolic capital are "attained when individuals act in ways that reliably demonstrate lack of interest in material acquisition by engaging in conspicuous consumption or conspicuous generosity" (Bliege-Bird & Smith, 2005: 223). In the context of strategic followership, it manifests when followers act in ways that reliably demonstrate subordination of self-interest and are illustrative of conspicuous generosity. The value of the display in terms of its symbolic capital lies in the cost of the investment in terms of time, energy, or other resources

30 *Strategic Role*

(Bliege-Bird & Smith, 2005; Turner, 1991). In other words, it is the value in excess of that generated by the good leader or what in economic terms is value premium. The subordination of interest is tantamount to over-riding self-gain to achieve superior value. As Bourdieu (1997) indicates, symbolic capital that results from prestige may be freely converted from one form to another, ultimately in order to gain advantages in the form of power, partners, and additional value.

Symbolic interaction examines the meanings derived from the reciprocal interaction of followers in the social environment with leaders. It focuses on the question, 'Which symbols and meanings emerge from the interaction between followers and leaders?' Symbolic interaction is a process including the interpretation of actions because symbolic meanings might be formed differently for followers. The followers interpret gestures (indications) and act on the basis of the interpreted meaning. They ascertain the meaning of the leaders' actions and convey indications to other relational constituents or even the leader as to how he or she is to act. This response can manifest in restorative situations where the meanings center on the bad behaviors of the leader and the indications of potential response center on appropriate restorative behaviors. Please note that in transcendent situations, the interpretations focus on the suboptimality of the good behaviors of the leader and likely behaviors that can generate optimal value for the relational constituents. Symbolic interaction is thus a process that includes the interpretation of actions because symbolic meanings might be formed differently for anyone.

Accurate interpretations result in valuable outcomes and lead to what might be termed symbolic capital, the resources available to the follower on the basis of honor, prestige or recognition, and serves as the value that he or she holds within relational context (Bliege-Bird & Smith, 2005). Symbolic capital is important in restorative and transcendent contexts because it enables followers to generate strategic value. Paul (1996: 82) "describes leader-follower interactions in a symbolic interactionism framework" and suggests that "the meaning placed on leader behaviors by followers is of importance in understanding the process by which leaders influence followers." He concludes that "symbolic leadership can influence followers' meaning-making processes in three ways: through the creation of shared meaning, through the creation of equifinal meaning, or through the creation of idiosyncratic meaning" Paul (1996, p. 82). DeRue and Ashford (2010) drew from social interaction (Blumer, 1969), a variant of symbolic interaction, to offer "a constructionist view that identifies leadership and followership as co-constructed in an interactive and reciprocal identity 'claiming' and 'granting' process." With respect to followership, DeRue and Ashford (2010) acknowledge that granting involves some individuals taking on follower roles to effectuate the construction of leadership.

Strategic Role 31

Studies using symbolic interactionism to examine followership focus primarily on operational followership (Zoogah, 2014). However, the theory can be applied at the strategic level through symbolic capital. The accumulation of symbolic capital is just as significant as the construction of meaning between the leader and the follower, particularly since such capital can be converted from one form to another, ultimately in order to gain advantages in the form of additional wealth, power, allies, and partners. Bourdieu (1977, 1990) suggests that the highest profits in symbolic capital are attained when individuals act in ways that reliably demonstrate a lack of interest in material acquisition by engaging in conspicuous generosity. The value of the display in terms of its symbolic capital lies in the cost of the investment in terms of time, energy, or wealth (Turner, 1991). The manifestation of symbolic capital (which tends to be very expensive in economic terms) increases the follower's social standing by displaying the quality of his or her capabilities, which is, in turn, linked to the attributes of his or her role. The resultant high social standing allows the follower to acquire powerful additional capital and to demonstrate his or her ability to defend and preserve the relationship for a long time.

Similarly, political theory can be employed to examine transcendent followership. In their role, politicians are representatives of their constituents. Politicians, as followers, are expected to bring home the bacon to their constituents who may be considered leaders. In their attempts, the politicians may inadvertently harm the very constituents they represent. It manifests through the interest-group paradox, which is the assertion that the demand for government programs (e.g., pork-barrel projects; tax credits and deductions, etc.) to benefit the constituents may, in fact, yield greater costs instead. A politician has to overcome this challenge if he or she is to generate extraordinary outcomes. One could therefore investigate the degree to which a particular politician is deemed transcendent by a constituency that may have paradoxically been a victim. This question focuses on the extent to which the politician overcame the paradox of interest to generate meaningful outcomes.

Summary

In sum, strategic role theory is concerned with the study of strategic behaviors that are characteristic of followers within strategic situational contexts and with various processes that presumably produce, explain, or are affected by those behaviors. Thus, the theoretical lenses discussed earlier have micro-level applications. They can be deployed in the study of followers as strategic resources to leaders, regulators of bad leaders, directors of inexperienced leaders, purveyors or informants of insular leaders, governors of leader–follower exchanges, representatives of effective leaders, reporters of high-performing leaders, boundary-spanners to

32 Strategic Role

sequestered leaders, investors to irresponsible leaders, recruiters to ineffective leaders, supporters of aspiring leaders, custodians of authentic leaders, counselors of traditional or conservative leaders, and challengers or competitors of underperforming leaders. Strategy can be imposed, realized or not; it can also be intended or materialized as an outcome.

Strategic management theories that implicitly and explicitly specify the role context of followership present opportunities to examine strategic followership. Some theories may be more suited to restorative followership while others are more suited to transcendent followership, and still others are suitable for both restorative and transcendent followership. The empirics determine the specific theory or theories to be deployed. Some might be integrated to effectively answer a question or extend our knowledge of strategic followership beyond what is already known.

Notes

1. www.oed.com/view/Entry/1938?rskey=eDo8os&result=1&isAdvanced=true#eid19916772.
2. www.dictionary.com/browse/stratagem.

References

Akerlof, G. (1970). The market for lemons: Qualitative uncertainty and the market mechanism. *Quarterly Journal of Economics*, 84(3).
Andersson, L. M., & Bateman T. S. (2000). Individual environmental initiative: Championing natural environmental issues in U.S. business organizations. *Academy of Management Journal*, 43, 548–570.
Ashford, S. J., & Cummings, L. L. (1985). Proactive feedback seeking: The instrumental use of the information environment. *Journal of Occupational Psychology*, 58(1), 67–79.
Barney, J. B. (1986). Organizational culture: Can it be a source of sustained competitive advantage? *Academy of Management Review*, 11(3), 656–665.
Bass, B. M., & Steidlmeier, P. (1999). Ethics, character, and authentic transformational leadership behavior. *The Leadership Quarterly*, 10(2), 181–217.
Bateman, T. S., & Porath, C. (2003). Transcendent behavior. In Cameron, K. S., Dutton, J. E. & Quinn, R. E. (Eds.), *Positive Organizational Scholarship: Foundations of a New Discipline* (pp. 122–137). San Francisco: Berrett-Koehler.
Biddle, B. J. (1979). *Role Theory: Expectations, Identities, and Behaviors* (p. 1). New York: Academic Press.
Blass, T. (2009). From new haven to Santa Clara: A historical perspective on the Milgram obedience experiments. *American Psychologist*, 64(1), 37.
Bliege-Bird, R., & Smith, E. A. (2005). Signaling theory, strategic interaction, and symbolic capital. *Current Anthropology*, 46(2), 221–248.
Bligh, M. C. (2011). Followership and follower-centered approaches. In A. Bryman, D. Collinson, K. Grint, B. Jackson, & M. Uhl-Bien (Eds.), *The Sage Handbook of Leadership* (pp. 393–403). London: Sage Publications.
Blumer, H. (1969). Fashion: From class differentiation to collective selection. *The Sociological Quarterly*, 10(3), 275–291.

Boino, M. C. (1999). Citizenship and impression management: Good soldiers or good actors? *Academy of Management Review*, 24(1), 82–98.

Boone, J. L. (1998). The evolution of magnanimity. *Human Nature*, 9(1), 1–21.

Boudreau, K. J., Lacetera, N., & Lakhani, K. R. (2011). Incentives and problem uncertainty in innovation contests: An empirical analysis. *Management Science*, 57(5), 843–863.

Bourdieu, P. (1977). The economics of linguistic exchanges. *Information (International Social Science Council)*, 16(6), 645–668.

Bourdieu, P. (1990). *The Logic of Practice*. Stanford University Press.

Bourdieu, P. (1997). Selections from the logic of practice. In *The Logic of the Gift: Toward an Ethic of Generosity* (pp. 190–230).

Brodbeck, F. C., Kerschreiter, R., Mojzisch, A., & Schulz-Hardt, S. (2007). Group decision making under conditions of distributed knowledge: The information asymmetries model. *Academy of Management Review*, 32(2), 459–479.

Burger, J. M. (2009). Replicating Milgram: Would people still obey today? *American Psychologist*, 64(1), 1.

Caldwell, C., Karri, R., & Vollmar, P. (2006). Principal theory and principle theory: Ethical governance from the follower's perspective. *Journal of Business Ethics*, 66(2–3), 207–223.

Cameron, K. S., & Whetten, D. A. (1983). Organizational effectiveness: One model or several? In Cameron, K. S. & Whetten, D. A. (Eds.), *Organizational Effectiveness: A Comparison of Multiple Models* (pp. 1–24). New York: Academic Press.

Carsten, M. K., & Uhl-Bien, M. (2012). Follower beliefs in the co-production of leadership: Examining upward communication and the moderating role of context. *Zeitschrift für Psychologie*, 220, 210–220.

Carsten, M. K., & Uhl-Bien, M. (2013). Ethical followership: An examination of followership beliefs and crimes of obedience. *Journal of Leadership & Organizational Studies*, 20(1), 49–61.

Carsten, M., Uhl-Bien, M., & Jaywickrema, A. (2013). "Reversing the lens" in leadership research: Investigating follower role orientation and leadership outcomes. Presented at the Southern Management Association (SMA) Annual Meeting, New Orleans, Louisiana.

Carsten, M. K., Uhl-Bien, M., West, B. J., Patera, J. L., & McGregor, R. (2010). Exploring social constructions of followership: A qualitative study. *The Leadership Quarterly*, 21.

Chaleff, I. (1995). *The Courageous Follower*. San Francisco: Berrett-Koehler.

Chaleff, I. (2003). *The Courageous Follower* (2nd ed.). San Francisco: Berrett-Koehler.

Chaleff, I. (2008). Creating new ways of following. In *The Art of Followership: How Great Followers Create Great Leaders and Organizations* (p. 146).

Chandler, A. D. (1962). Strategy and structure: Chapters in the history of the American enterprise. *Massachusetts Institute of Technology Cambridge*, 4(2), 125–137.

Connelly, B. L., Tihanyi, L., Crook, T. R., & Gangloff, K. A. (2014). Tournament theory: Thirty years of contests and competitions. *Journal of Management*, 40(1), 16–47.

De Cremer, D., & Van Dijk, E. (2005). When and why leaders put themselves first: Leader behaviour in resource allocations as a function of feeling entitled. *European Journal of Social Psychology*, 35(4), 553–563.

34 Strategic Role

Dechenaux, E., Kovenock, D., & Sheremeta, R. M. (2015). A survey of experimental research on contests, all-pay auctions and tournaments. *Experimental Economics*, 18(4), 609–669.

DeRue, D. S., & Ashford, S. J. (2010). Who will lead and who will follow? A social process of leadership identity construction in organizations. *Academy of Management Review*, 35(4), 627–647.

Dvir, T., & Shamir, B. (2003). Follower developmental characteristics as predicting transformational leadership: A longitudinal field study. *The Leadership Quarterly*, 14(3), 327–344.

Epitropaki, O., Sy, T., Martin, R., Tram-Quon, S., & Topakas, A. (2013). Implicit leadership and followership theories "in the wild": Taking stock of information-processing approaches to leadership and followership in organizational settings. *The Leadership Quarterly*, 24(6), 858–881.

Feldman, M. (2000). Organizational routines as a source of continuous change. *Organization Science*, 11(6), 611–629.

Felin, T., & Foss, N. J. (2009). Organizational routines and capabilities: Historical drift and a course-correction toward microfoundations. *Scandinavian Journal of Management*, 25(2), 157–167.

Foss, N. J., & Lindenberg, S. (2013). Microfoundations for strategy: A goal-framing perspective on the drivers of value creation. *Academy of Management Perspectives*, 27(2), 85–102.

French, J., & Raven, B. (1959). The basis of social power. In Cartwright, D. (Ed.), *Studies in social power* (pp. 150–167). Ann Arbor: University of Michigan, Institute for Social Research.

Frese, M., & Fay, D. (2001). Personal initiative: An active performance concept for work in the 21st century. *Research in Organizational Behavior*, 23, 133–187.

Frooman, J. (1999). Stakeholder influence strategies. *Academy of Management Review*, 24(2), 191–205.

Gintis, H., Smith, E. A., & Bowles, S. (2001). Costly signaling and cooperation. *Journal of Theoretical Biology*, 213(1), 103–119.

Golembiewski, R. T. (2000). Stakeholders in consultation. *Public Administration and Public Policy*, 81, 529–534.

Graen, G. B., & Uhl-Bien, M. (1995). Relationship-based approach to leadership: Development of leader-member exchange (LMX) theory of leadership over 25 years: Applying a multi-level multi-domain perspective. *The Leadership Quarterly*, 6(2), 219–247.

Grant, A. M., & Ashford, S. J. (2008). The dynamics of proactivity at work. *Research in Organizational Behavior*, 28, 3–34.

Grant, A. M., Parker, S., & Collins, C. (2009). Getting credit for proactive behavior: Supervisor reactions depend on what you value and how you feel. *Personnel Psychology*, 62(1), 31–55.

Heckscher, C. (1994). In Heckscher, Charles & Donnellon, Anne (Eds.), *Defining the Post-Bureaucratic Type in the Post-Bureaucratic Organization* (pp. 14–62). Thousand Oaks, CA: Sage Publication.

Hollander, E. P. (1974). Processes of leadership emergence. *Journal of Contemporary Business*, 3(4), 19–33.

Hollander, E. P. (1993). Legitimacy, power and influence: A perspective on relational features of leadership. In Chemers, M. M. & Ayman, R. (Eds.), *Leadership Theory and Research: Perspectives and Directions* (pp. 29–48). San Diego: Academic Press.

Hoption, C., Christie, A., & Barling, J. (2012). Submitting to the follower label: Followership, positive affect, and extra-role behaviors. *Zeitschrift für Psychologie*, 220(4), 221–230.

Horwath, R. (2006). The origin of strategy. *Strategic Thinking Institute*, 1–5.

Howell, J. P., & Mendez, M. (2008). Three perspectives on followership. In *The Art of Followership: How Great Followers Create Great Leaders and Organizations* (Vol. 146, pp. 25–39). Boston, MA: Harvard Business Publishing.

Howell, J. M., & Shamir, B. (2005). The role of followers in the charismatic leadership process: Relationships and their consequences. *Academy of Management Review*, 30(1), 96–112.

Keller, K. L. (2008). *Best Practice Cases in Branding: Lessons From the World's Strongest Brands*. Englewood Cliffs, NJ: Prentice Hall.

Kellerman, B. (2008). *Followership: How Followers Are Creating Change and Changing Leaders*. Boston: Harvard Business School Press.

Kelley, R. (1992). *The Power of Followership*. New York: Doubleday.

Kelly, R. E. (1988). In praise of followers. *Harvard Business Review*, November–December, 142–148.

King, A. J., Johnson, D. D., & Van Vugt, M. (2009). The origins and evolution of leadership. *Current Biology*, 19(19), R911–R916.

Kipnis, D., Schmidt, S. M., & Wilkinson, I. (1980). Intraorganizational influence tactics: Explorations in getting one's way. *Journal of Applied Psychology*, 65(4), 440.

Kirmani, A., & Rao, A. R. (2000). No pain, no gain: A critical review of the literature on signaling unobservable product quality. *Journal of Marketing*, 64(2), 66–79.

Lazear, E. P., & Rosen, S. (1981). Rank-order tournaments as optimum labor contracts. *Journal of Political Economy*, 89(5), 841–864.

Lipman-Blumen, J. (2005). Toxic leadership: When grand illusions masquerade as noble visions. *Leader to Leader*, 2005(36), 29–36.

Louis, M. (1983). Organizations as culture-bearing milieux. In Pondy, L., Frost, P., Morgan, G., & Dandridge, T. (Eds.), *Organizational Symbolism* (pp. 186–218). Greenwich, CT: JAI Press.

Maak, T., & Pless, N. M. (2006). Responsible leadership in a stakeholder society—A relational perspective. *Journal of Business Ethics*, 66(1), 99–115.

Matthews, J. A & Cho, D. S. (2000). *Tiger Technology: The Creating of a Semiconductor Industry in East Asia*. Cambridge: Cambridge University Press.

Messersmith, J. G., Guthrie, J. P., Ji, Y. Y., & Lee, J. Y. (2011). Executive turnover: The influence of dispersion and other pay system characteristics. *Journal of Applied Psychology*, 96(3), 457.

Millet, K., & Dewitte, S. (2007). Altruistic behavior as a costly signal of general intelligence. *Journal of Research in Personality*, 41(2), 316–326.

Mintzberg, H. (1998). Covert leadership: Notes on managing professionals. *Harvard Business Review*, 76, 140–148.

36 *Strategic Role*

Morrison, E. W. (2006). Doing the job well: An investigation of pro-social rule breaking. *Journal of Management*, 32(1), 5–28.

Morrison, E. W., & Milliken, F. J. (2000). Organizational silence: A barrier to change and development in a pluralistic world. *Academy of Management Review*, 25(4), 706–725.

Morrison, E. W., & Phelps, C. C. (1999). Taking charge at work: Extrarole efforts to initiate workplace change. *Academy of Management Journal*, 42(4), 403–419.

Neiman, F. D. (1998). Conspicuous consumption as wasteful advertising: a Darwinian perspective on spatial patterns in Classic Maya terminal monument dates. In Barton C. M. & Clark G. A. (Eds.), *Rediscovering Darwin: Evolutionary Theory and Archeological Explanation. Archeological Papers of the American Anthropological Association, No. 7* (pp. 267–290). Washington, DC: American Anthropological Association.

Nilsson, W. (2015). Positive institutional work: Exploring institutional work through the lens of positive organizational scholarship. *Academy of Management Review*, 40(3), 370–398.

North, D. C. (1990). A transaction cost theory of politics. *Journal of Theoretical Politics*, 2(4), 355–367.

Offermann, L. R., Kennedy Jr, J. K., & Wirtz, P. W. (1994). Implicit leadership theories: Content, structure, and generalizability. *The Leadership Quarterly*, 5(1), 43–58.

Ornstein, S. (1986). Organizational symbols: A study of their meanings and influences on perceived psychological climate. *Organizational Behavior and Human Decision Processes*, 38(2), 207–229.

Parker, S. K., Williams, H. M., & Turner, N. (2006). Modeling the antecedents of proactive behavior at work. *Journal of Applied Psychology*, 91(3), 636–652.

Parker, S. K., Wall, T. D., & Jackson, P. R. (1997). "That's not my job": Developing flexible employee work orientations. *Academy of Management Journal*, 40(4), 899–929.

Paul, J. (1996). A symbolic interactionist perspective on leadership. *Journal of Leadership and Organizational Studies*, (2), 82–93.

Pfeffer, J. (1998). *The Human Equation: Building Profits by Putting People First.* Boston: Harvard Business School Press.

Pless, N. M., & Maak, T. (2011). Responsible leadership: Pathways to the future. In *Responsible Leadership* (pp. 3–13). Dordrecht: Springer.

Rosen, S. (1986). The theory of equalizing differences. *Handbook of Labor Economics*, 1, 641–692.

Ross, J. M., & Sharapov, D. (2015). When the leader follows: Avoiding dethronement through imitation. *Academy of Management Journal*, 58(3), 658–679.

Rost, J. 2008. Followership: An outmoded concept. In Riggio, R. E., Chaleff, I., & Lipman-Blumen, J. (Eds.), *The Art of Followership: How Great Followers Create Great Leaders and Organizations.* San Francisco, CA: Jossey-Bass.

Schneider, M. (2002). A stakeholder model of organizational leadership. *Organization Science*, 13(2), 209–220.

Scott, W. R. (2014). *Institutions and Organizations* (4th ed.). London, UK: Sage Publication.

Seip, K. L., & Grøn, Ø. (2016). Leading the game, losing the competition: Identifying leaders and followers in a repeated game. *PloS One*, 11(3), e0150398.

Shamir, B. (2007). From passive recipients to active co-producers: Followers' roles in the leadership process. Follower-centered perspectives on leadership: A tribute to the memory of James R. *Meindl*, 9–39.

Shapiro, A. L. (1999). *The Control Revolution: How the Internet is Putting Individuals in Charge and Changing the World We Know*. New York: Perseus Books.

Sharapov, D., & Ross, J. M. (2015). Whom should a leader imitate in multiple competitor settings? A contingency perspective. In *Academy of Management Proceedings* (Vol. 2015, No. 1, p. 18068). Briarcliff Manor, NY: Academy of Management.

Shogren, J. F., & Baik, K. H. (1992). Favorites and underdogs: Strategic behavior in an experimental contest. *Public Choice*, 74(2), 191–205.

Smircich, L. (1983). Concepts of culture and organizational analysis. *Administrative Science Quarterly*, 339–358.

Stech, E. L. (2008). A new Leadership-followership paradigm. In Riggio, R. E., Chaleff, I., & Lipman-Blumen, J. (Eds.), *The Art of Followership: How Great Followers Create Great Leaders and Organizations* (J-B Warren Bennis Series). San Francisco, CA: Jossey-Bass.

Stiglitz, J. E. (1977). Monopoly, non-linear pricing and imperfect information: The insurance market. *The Review of Economic Studies*, 44(3), 407–430.

Sy, T. (2010). What do you think of followers? Examining the content, structure, and consequences of implicit followership theories. *Organizational Behavior and Human Decision Processes*, 113(2), 73–84.

Sy, T. (2011). *I Think, Therefore I Do: Influence of Leaders' and Followers' Implicit Followership Theories on Relationship Quality and Follower Performance*. San Antonio, TX: Academy of Management.

Tepper, B. J., Duffy, M. K., Henle, C. A., & Lambert, L. S. (2006). Procedural injustice, victim precipitation, and abusive supervision. *Personnel Psychology*, 59(1), 101–123.

Tepper, B. J., Duffy, M. K., & Shaw, J. D. (2001). Personality moderators of the relationship between abusive supervision and subordinates' resistance. *Journal of Applied Psychology*, 86(5), 974.

Tourish, D. (2014). Leadership, more or less? A processual, communication perspective on the role of agency in leadership theory. *Leadership*, 10(1), 79–98.

Turner, T. S. (1991). Representing, resisting rethinking: Historical formation of Kayapo culture and anthropological consciousness. In Stocking Jr., George W. (Ed), *Colonial Situations. Essay on the Contextualization of Ethnographic Knowledge* (pp. 285–313). Milwaukee: University of Wisconsin Press.

Tzu, S. (1971). *The Art of War*, translated and with an introduction by Samuel B. Griffith. London, UK: Oxford University Press.

Uhl-Bien, M., Riggio, R. E., Lowe, K. B., & Carsten, M. K. (2014). Followership theory: A review and research agenda. *The Leadership Quarterly*, 25(1), 83–104.

38   Strategic Role

Uken, B. (2008). Followership in a professional services firm. In *The Art of Followership How Great Followers Create Great Leaders and Organizations* (pp. 127–136). Boston, MA: Harvard Business Publishing.

Van Dyne, L., & LePine, J. A. (1998). Helping and voice extra-role behaviors: Evidence of construct and predictive validity. *Academy of Management Journal*, 41(1), 108–119.

Van Vugt, M., Hogan, R., & Kaiser, R. B. (2008). Leadership, followership, and evolution: Some lessons from the past. *American Psychologist*, 63(3), 182.

Weber, M. (1968). *On Charisma and Institution Building*. Chicago: University of Chicago Press.

Whiting, S. W., Maynes, T. D., Podsakoff, N. P., & Podsakoff, P. M. (2012). Effects of message, source, and context on evaluations of employee voice behavior. *Journal of Applied Psychology*, 97(1), 159.

Williamson, O. E. (1979). Transaction-cost economics: The governance of contractual relations. *The Journal of Law and Economics*, 22(2), 233–261.

Williamson, O. E. (2000). The new institutional economics: Taking stock, looking ahead. *Journal of Economic Literature*, 38(3), 595–613.

Zajac, E. J. (1990). CEO selection, succession, compensation and firm performance: A theoretical integration and empirical analysis. *Strategic Management Journal*, 11(3), 217–230.

Zaleznik, A. (1965). The dynamics of subordinacy. *Harvard Business Review*, 43(3), 119–131.

Zoogah, D. B. (2006). *Alliance mental models and strategic alliance team effectiveness* (Doctoral dissertation, The Ohio State University).

Zoogah, D. B. (2014). *Strategic Followership: How Followers Impact Organizational Effectiveness*. New York, NY: Palgrave Macmillan.

3 Strategic Situations

How do strategic situations and their changes influence outcomes of strategic followership? The leadership literature shows situations as one major determinant of the leader–follower exchange. Recently, there has been a distinction between psychological and strategic situations. The latter are proposed as major determinants of strategic followership (see Zoogah, 2014). Studies of strategic followership therefore require an understanding of the theoretical lens that facilitates an understanding of strategic situations. Another characteristic of the leader–follower transactions is dynamics. As a result, I focus on strategic dynamics. Not only do the behaviors and cognitive orientations of leaders and followers change, but also the structure and progression of the relationships change. Given the centrality of dynamics in relational exchanges, it seems important to discuss theoretical lenses for studying strategic dynamics.

3.1 Strategic Context

The social sciences emphasize the significance of context, the physical, psychological, and institutional features that provide meaning to the specific descriptors that elucidate strategic roles (Rousseau & Fried, 2001; Mischel & Shoda, 2010). Institutional (Scott, 2014) and economic exchange theories (Williamson, 1985) suggest that individuals and firms have to adapt to their environments. Adaptation, the basis for strategic behavior (Oliver, 1991) and governance of firm operations (Williamson, 1991), is a function of the external and internal environments (Lele, 1992). Firms may adapt to opportunities or threats in the environment or based on their strengths and weaknesses. The influence interface (leader–follower exchange, where a follower has the capacity to persuade the leader to go along with what the follower wants and intends of the leader's own volition) is equally characterized by an external environment that proffers opportunities for, and threats against, value maximization (Zoogah, 2014). Similarly, the internal environment defines the unique attributes of firms as strengths and weakness of the following firm such that through discernment, a follower is able to calculate the probability of achieving

40 Strategic Situations

its strategic objectives. The combination of these two dimensions yields four strategic contexts—strategic leverage, strategic constraint, strategic vulnerability, and strategic problem—for adaptation.

3.1.1 Strategic Leverage

The concept of leverage is common in finance, market, operations, and management (Matsa, 2010). In management it generally refers to the use of some instrument or asset to maximum advantage. As a result, it is often linked to strategy. For example, Lipparini and Sobrero (1994) argue that the competitiveness that emerges as a network-embedded capability and the coordination among firms, maximizing firm-specific competencies, represents a strategic leverage in accomplishing and maintaining a sustainable competitive advantage. Lele (1992) proposes that firms can match company strengths with market opportunities to create strategic leverage. He defined strategic leverage as a company's maneuver (its ability to change its competitive position in a market) multiplied by its return (changes in revenue, market share, or both that result from any maneuver). In this book, I define strategic leverage as a following firm's ability to influence a leading firm to achieve superior outcomes consistent with the fundamental objectives of the constituents in the relationship exchange. To the extent that a following firm discerns its leverage, the firm is likely to engage in behaviors that enable achievement of its strategic outcomes.

Strategic leverage is thus a capability that enables a firm actor to achieve some outcomes. The environment surrounding the influence exchange proffers opportunities to the firms and, given their strengths, leverage to take advantage of those opportunities to advance their objectives. Ross and Sharapov (2015) observe that "the response delay inherent in imitating the follower's position in the face of uncertainty provides an opportunity to the follower to catch up with the leader" (p. 675). High uncertain situations may completely deter the leading firm from switching positions, which enables the following firm to achieve superior outcomes (Ross & Sharapov, 2015). Strategic leverage may also arise from norms regulating the relational exchange of the firms. Symbolic interactionalism (Mead, 1934) and modes of social interaction (Goffman, 1974) demonstrate that the active interaction between firms relies on symbols, meaningful information, and social norms that help to define the context and nature of the relationship. Social norms are the regulative mechanisms most relevant to the leader–follower relationship; they specify the standards or rules of acceptable behavior. For example, social norms inhibit followers from overtly challenging their leaders (Courpasson & Dany, 2003) or damaging the relationship (Glauser, 1984; Milliken, Morrison, & Hewlin, 2003; Tynan, 2005) in a way that harms both parties. Since norms focus on the relationship they enable following firms to behave for the collective good (at least the benefit of each firm).

3.1.2 Strategic Constraint

In strategic constraint contexts, firms are not able to take advantage of opportunities in the relational environment because of their weaknesses. Strategic constraint thus refers to the degree to which a firm is limited in its ability to exploit gains from its operations, interactions, and systems because of a lack of potential (Hull & Lio, 2006). It is similar to Spector's (2011) theory of constraint, which argues that the business model a company uses can limit its ability to exploit opportunities. Coman and Ronen (2007) define strategic constraint as the limitations influencing a firm's business arena; they argue for management of such constraints through a series of steps: (1) identifying the arena constraint and its migration path, (2) creating a vision for navigating the firm toward an advantageous position in the business arena, and (3) translating that vision into a program for realigning the firm's structure and priorities. Strategic constraints determine what a firm can do when faced with a number of options that it might consider. The external circumstances and the nature of the firm's resources, for example, are typical strategic constraints (Barney, 1991; Child, 1972, 1975).

Strategic constraints here refer to the hurdles a following firm might encounter in the relational exchange. Behavioral uncertainty (e.g., lack of trust) functions as a strategic constraint because it creates a strategic order (actors' sense of their own knowledge as a condition for defining their own strategies and preferences) and a relational order (e.g., actors' sense of the party's knowledge as a condition for repositioning and reorienting their own preferences and strategies with regard to it). To the extent that the following firm can influence factors of a strategic and relational order in the exchange the firm (or individual) is likely to adjust or adapt well or break out of adaptive behavior. Of course, exogenous and endogenous factors, defined by the behaviors of the following firm in the exchange, may drive the actors to interpret the situation as a framework for developing a strategic-relationally 'appropriate' behavior. Constraint induces reliance on the part of the weak party (i.e., leading firm) to depend on the following firm. That dependence may drive strategic behaviors of one or both firms to optimize outcomes.

3.1.3 Strategic Vulnerability

The *Merriam-Webster Dictionary* (2014) defines *vulnerability* as a "state of being exposed." It has both positive (natural hazards and crisis management literature—Wisner, Blaikie, Cannon, & Davis, 2004) and negative (sustainability science literature) connotations. In the strategic management literature, it refers to the "susceptibility of a firm to business condition or situation that lowers performance" (Jain & Singal, 2014: 42). Vulnerability differs from risk and disruption (Jain & Singal, 2014).

42 Strategic Situations

It has been approached from diverse views including market positioning, resource-based view, organizational ecology, organizational evolution, and organizational theory. Whitehead, Blair, Smith, Nix, and Savage (1989) find that Health Management Organizations (HMOs) are strategically vulnerable on the social dimension of stakeholder supportiveness because of their dependence on the stakeholders. Spekman (1988) also finds that buyers who perceive varying levels of strategic vulnerability differ in their reliance on sources of information and in their evaluation of supplier/product characteristics.

Strategic vulnerability here refers to the inability of a following firm, despite its strengths, to achieve desired strategic outcomes because of threats in the external environment. Threat, a key variable in organization–environment–strategy relationships, manifests through power. Power is a function of the dependence of one organization on another in the context of followership exchanges. To the extent that a following firm depends on a leading firm for tangible and intangible resources, it is likely the former will be vulnerable, which could cause it to engage in actions that do not contribute value. For example, the following firm may not engage in behaviors that restore any value diminished as a result of the leading firm's actions. In other words, the leading firm is likely to control the following firm in undesirable ways. To counteract the control, the following firm may avoid the leading firm that, although strategically consistent, nonetheless undermines the relational exchange and negatively affects their images. It is also possible the strategic vulnerability leads to strategic behaviors that yield positive long-term outcomes.

3.1.4 Strategic Problem

Firms typically seek to achieve certain strategic outcomes. Problems arise when the external environment is threatening and the firm is weak. As in strategic vulnerability where threat makes an actor susceptible to some conditions that lower performance, firms that are weak and face threats have problems. A strategic problem generally is complex and ill structured because of bounded rationality, self-interest seeking with guile, heterogeneous information, knowledge, and motivation (Baer, Dirks, & Nickerson, 2013; Lyles & Mitroff, 1980). Baer, Dirks, and Nickerson (2012, p. 199) define a strategic problem as "a deviation from a desired set of specific or a range of acceptable conditions resulting in a symptom or a web of symptoms recognized as needing to be addressed" (e.g., Cowan, 1986; Newell & Simon, 1972).

A strategic problem thus refers to the inability of a following firm to achieve desired strategic outcomes due to threats in the relational environment and the weakness of that firm. A firm has a strategic problem when it lacks the competence or capability to make a valuable contribution because of the perceived threat of the interacting firm or its own weaknesses. Strategic followership assumes that the follower has the competence to make a significant contribution (Zoogah, 2014). To the extent that the following firm cannot make a contribution to its strategic objectives, it is saddled with a strategic problem.

In sum, the strategic contexts—leverage, vulnerability, constraint, and problem—define not only the patterns of relating between firms (Hardy & Phillips, 1998) but also the influence dynamics. According to Fiske (1993) there are communal-sharing, authority-ranking, equality-matching, and market-pricing relationships. Interfirm relationships are characterized by the latter two while interpersonal relationships are characterized by the former two. In these latter two, there is no authority between the firms, but there is collaboration around shared goals and helping one another on the basis of appeals or a loose exchange of favors. In addition to this equality-matching attribute, the relationship may be based around a specific transaction where substantive items are exchanged between the firms. While leverage and vulnerability situations may be associated with equality-matching patterns, constraint and problem situations might be associated with market-pricing relationships. The influence dynamics in equality matching is based on appeals or loose exchanges while that of the market pricing is based on transactions or hard exchanges. The strategic context thus affects the strategic interactions of a following firm and a leading firm. Even though the focus of strategic context here is at the firm level, the components—strategic leverage, strategic constraint, strategic vulnerability, and strategic problem—also apply to individuals. At the interpersonal level, the external and internal relational environments present opportunities, threats, strengths, and weaknesses for individual followers.

3.2 Theories of Strategic Situations

3.2.1 Game Theory

The first theory of strategic situations is game theory. Games are basically a taxonomy of strategic situations. Game theory, "the study of mathematical models of conflict and cooperation between intelligent rational decision-makers" (Myerson, 1993: vii–xi), is primarily used in economics, political science, psychology, and management, as well as logic, computer science, and biology. Game theory applies to a wide range of behavioral relations with regard to logical decision-making in humans, animals, and computers. Behavioral game theory specifically focuses on predicting human behavior in strategic situations. Even though there are several types of games, cooperative games seem appropriate in strategic followership. A game is cooperative if a follower and a leader are able to form binding commitments externally enforced (e.g. through contracts). A contract here refers to the social norms implicit in followership and leadership roles. Because analysis of cooperative games focuses on predicting which coalitions will emerge, the joint actions that groups take and the resulting group payoffs, such games seem appropriate for

44   *Strategic Situations*

transcendent followership. A game is noncooperative if followers and leaders cannot collaborate or implicit agreements are self-enforcing (e.g. through credible threats). In restorative followership, where the expectations and behaviors of the follower counter those of the leader, cooperation between the leader and follower seems unlikely or impossible. The follower enacts restorative behaviors through self-imposed (e.g., moral) binding commitment. The noncooperative games focus on predicting individual players' actions and payoffs. So, they seem more appropriate in restorative followership.

Cooperative games describe the structure, strategies, and payoffs of coalitions. It is therefore possible to investigate the relational structure of strategic followers and leaders in transcendent context. For example, what strategies are adopted by strategic followers to maximize payoffs either to the leader, department or organization. Different payoffs are associated with different strategies and relational constituents. Non-cooperative games that look at how bargaining procedures will affect the distribution of payoffs within each specific strategic situation can be adopted in restorative followership situations because of the risks associated with restoration.

The leadership literature shows situations as one major determinant of the leader–follower exchange. Given that strategic situation is a major determinant of strategic followership (Zoogah, 2014), studies of strategic followership therefore require an understanding of the theoretical lens that facilitate the study of strategic situations. A situation is strategic if it presents a dilemma and requires a choice (Zoogah, 2014). In the language of game theory, strategic situations require strategic moves. In other words, they present a sequence of choices faced by a follower along with what he or she knows when the person chooses to respond to the behavior of a leader. A strategic situation involves three elements: the decision-maker (i.e., follower), the strategy sets (i.e., over what he or she is making the decision), and payoffs (how he or she evaluates the different decisions). The broad categories of strategic situations a follower confronts are two: good and bad. He or she has to decide *who* to respond to the bad leadership behaviors (S_b) or good leadership behaviors (S_g). The set of situations are thus (A) $[S_b]$, (B) $[S_g]$, and (C) $[S_b + S_g]$. A represents bad leaders while B represents good leaders, and C represents leaders that are sometimes bad and other times good. The strategy sets in A, B, and C are different, and so are the payoffs. Situations in the C category are complex and involve mixed strategies and payoffs. This chapter therefore discusses some theories that might be used to study strategic followership situations. But first, I elaborate on the concept of strategic situation or context.

In the relational interface, the follower and the leader present dilemmatic situations for each other. The follower may decide to respond or not respond in much the same way that the leader may behave badly or not behave badly. If the follower decides to respond to the bad behavior

Strategic Situations   45

of a leader by restoring diminished value, the payoff (the intrinsic rewards in the form of satisfaction for doing good, living up to his or her moral code) will be greater than that of the leader. However, if the follower does not respond, then value diminishment may worsen and the follower may have a bad payoff (compunctions for not doing something). Of course, the non-response may be good because it does not incur the 'wrath' of the leader for trying to be a 'smarty-pant.' Consequently, the payoff is lower than if he/she responds to generate value. If the leader does not behave badly, there will be no value to be restored and no payoffs. So, both the leader and the follower have zero gains. Similarly, with no bad behavior, the nonresponse of the follower will not matter. Consequently, the gains will be zero. Thus, it seems that when a leader behaves badly, it is better for a follower to engage in restoring any diminished value.

Both the leader and the follower can behave badly (Kellerman, 2008) even though strategic followership focuses on the leader's behavior. Situation A shows a loss in value of 100 for each. In other words, both contribute less to the strategic outcomes of the relational constituents (e.g., organization). On the other hand, both can behave in a good way resulting in a gain in value of 100 by each. Situation B shows that both contribute to the strategic outcomes of the relational constituents. This symmetry is different from Situations C and D. In C the leader behaves badly but the follower enacts good behavior. It shows that while the leader decreases the value (–100) the follower increases the value (100). In D, it is the reverse: the follower decreases value (–100) while the leader increases value (100) (Figures 3.1–3.3).

		Follower Behavior	
		Bad	*Good*
Leader Behavior	*Bad*	(A) (–100, –100)	(C) (–100, 100)
	Good	(D) (100, –100)	(B) (100, 100)

Figure 3.1 General Strategic Situations

		Follower Response Behavior	
		Increase	*Decrease*
Bad Leader Behavior	*Increase*	(25%, 75%)	(25%, 75%)
	Decrease	(45%, 55%)	(45%, 55%)

Figure 3.2 Restorative Situations

46 Strategic Situations

Follower Response Behavior

		Increase	Decrease
Good Leader Behavior	Increase	(50%, 50%)	(55%, 45%)
	Decrease	(45%, 55%)	(50%, 50%)

Figure 3.3 Transcendent Situations

Strategic followership focuses on only positive outcomes (i.e., good behaviors) of followers. As a result, Situations A and D are not relevant. So, I focus on only B and C. In the latter, followers behave either restoratively and transcendently. In restorative situations (see Figure 3.2), the leader could increase his or her bad behavior and the follower may also increase his or her response behavior. The situations are assumed to contribute equally to value creation (Zoogah, 2014). So, the bad behavior of the leader could increase or decrease, and the restorative behavior of the follower could also increase or decrease. Increased bad behavior decreases the proportion of the leader's share while decreased bad behavior increases his or her share. Similarly, the response behavior of the follower increases the proportion of the follower's share, and decreased responses decreases his or her share.

In transcendent situations (see Figure 3.3), both the leader and the follower engage in good behaviors but the former is less than optimal (Zoogah, 2014). The follower's response behavior thus seeks to optimize the value to be generated by the relational actors. Put another way, the leader is leaving some value on the table, and the follower acts to ensure that the value is either not left on the table or increases. Increased good behavior of the leader and response of the follower result in equal shared contribution. However, when either decreases their good actions, the shared value is asymmetric.

What we have not considered is the payoff to the follower. Expressed as numbers in Table 3.1, the payoffs measure the utility or happiness index or satisfaction of a player (follower and leader in this case). Outcomes with higher numbers indicate the best outcomes. So, in Table 3.1, the outcomes with 5 are the best payoffs while those with 4 are the second-best payoffs, those with 3 are the third-best, those with 2 are the fourth-best, and those with 1 have the worst payoff. They suggest that followers who generate the best outcomes are those with 5s.

3.2.2 Culture Theory

It is now taken for granted that the values, beliefs, and behavioral norms that underlie organizations are instruments serving organizational needs,

Strategic Situations 47

Table 3.1 Bad leadership behavior and Payoffs

Outcome	Leader	(Aggrieved) Leader	Follower
No bad behavior	4	1	5
Bad behavior, restoration, negative consequence	2	4	3
Bad behavior, restoration, positive consequence	3	2	4
Bad behavior, no restoration, negative consequence	1	3	2
Bad behavior, no restoration, positive consequence	5	5	1

function as adaptative-regulatory mechanisms that unite individual members into organizational structures, and serve as systems of shared cognitions and shared symbols and meanings (Smircich, 1983). Values are social standards that guide behavior (Schwartz, 1992). In that regard, role occupants such as priests, pastors, or counselors who function as repositories of value to the specific organizational settings can be studied to understand their strategic roles. The organizational counselor has one of the most challenging tasks; he or she has to tread a very thin line between the organization and the individual in training, consulting, changing, informing, advocating, giving advice, and serving as a diplomat. How he or she maintains this role with clear demarcation lines, acceptable boundaries, and supportive relationships requires maturity and training. How organizations function as repositories of value can yield insight into that unique role particularly as it relates to organizational competitiveness. The role of a counselor is about ensuring not only that the values of the organization are sustained but also that they stimulate personal growth of the leader in the current relationship and the organization through decreased costs related to turnover, burnout, absenteeism, and accident-related disability; improvement in leader performance and increase in productivity; and resolution of behavioral problems arising from organizational changes. Such behaviors are proactive human resource strategies (Navare, 2008) that can be compared. To what extent a culture facilitates restorative and transcendent followership behaviors is an interesting question that needs to be explored empirically.

3.2.3 Organizational Routine Theory

The route of organizational routines began with Veblen (1898) and came through Schumpeter (1934) and Alchian (1950) to evolutionary economics (Parmigiani & Howard-Grenville, 2011). Nelson and Winter (1982) view evolution as gradual changes in routine-like behavior. From that point, evolutionary economics refers to the capabilities and practices of an organization as "the repertoires of organization members" that are "associated with the possession of particular collections" of resources,

48 *Strategic Situations*

including the ability to utilize those resources productively (Nelson & Winter, 1982: 103). It focuses on repetitive processes and systems that enable organizations to function and grow (Becker, 2004; Winter, 2005). Routines are thus variously defined as "pattern of behavior that is followed repeatedly, but is subject to change if conditions change" (Winter, 1964: 263); "flexible patterns offering a variety of alternative choices" (Koestler, 1967: 44); "generative systems with internal structures and dynamics" (Pentland & Feldman, 2005: 793); "ordered sets of actions" or "grammars of action" (Pentland & Rueter, 1994: 489); and "patterned sequences of learned behavior involving multiple actors who are linked by relations of communication and/or authority" (Cohen & Bacdayan, 1994: 555). While some (e.g., Becker, 2004) view routines as "patterns," it does not always seem clear whether these patterns denote nonobservable, individual level "habits of thought" or observable, individual level "habits" or even collective-level, nonobservable thought patterns or observable recurrent interaction patterns (Felin & Foss, 2009). Parmigiani and Howard-Grenville (2011) suggest two perspectives—practice and capabilities. The practice perspective emphasizes processes and focuses on "how routines are enacted in the day-to-day and with what consequences" (Parmigiani & Howard-Grenville, 2011: 417) while the practice routines, "repetitive, recognizable patterns of interdependent action, carried out by multiple actors" (Feldman & Pentland, 2003: 95), focus on the internal workings of specific processes in specific organizational contexts. The latter differs from the former that emphasizes the accomplishments of routines toward organizational goals. Capability routines are considered "the building blocks of capabilities, with a repetitive and context-dependent nature" (Dosi, Faillo, & Marengo, 2008: 1167).

How can organizational routines be applied to strategic followership? Subordinates often function in various roles that are routinized. In human resources management, for example, a recruiter engages in patterned activities toward the acquisition of skills and competencies for the organization. The recruiter also interacts with his or her supervisor in a patterned manner that matches the recruitment activities they have to deal with. In that regard their relationship is routinized for a specific purpose. Follower–leader exchanges can be considered routinized enabling the use of routine theory to understand not only the effectiveness of the routines but also the activities that bear on those routines. The practice and capability perspectives of routines may also be applied to strategic followership to understand how entities in that role contribute to the outcomes of relational constituents. Last, the patterns of restorative and transcendent behaviors may be studied to examine how they optimize value to relational constituents.

3.2.4 Symbolism Theory

Symbols are important facets of organizational life. They represent some value and convey particular meaning to individuals (Berg, 1986).

For example, organizational logos enable individuals to identify with organizations. Symbols are subjective elements of organizational life, and a different frame of reference but complement objective frames of reference in organizations (Dandrige, Mitroff, & Joyce, 1980). They also have some value that can be exchanged in the market (Berg, 1986). Berg (1986) suggests the management of symbolic resources, "symbols, metaphors, images, etc., which in a condensed form represent complex organizational phenomena, and which can be developed and utilized to guide strategic corporate action" (p. 557). He proffers four types of "symbolic resources"—historical resources (i.e., elements of the corporate saga or epic), basic values and ideologies (as expressed in the corporate policies), particular activities and events (as anniversaries and celebrations), and, finally, the company lifestyle (or ethos). The preservation and promotion of symbolic resources are behaviors that followers may engage in to create or sustain value to organizations. Dandrige et al. (1980) propose verbal, action, and material symbols, each of which has descriptive, energy-controlling, and system maintenance functions. Organizational symbolism theory suggests that organizational systems are significant in the functioning of organizational members to the extent that they provide meaning, value, sustenance, and identity (Berg, 1986; Dandrige et al., 1980; Pratt & Rafaelli, 1997).

In that regard, organizational symbolism has application to strategic followership. Organizations are patterns of symbolic discourse such that the organization is maintained through symbolic modes, such as language that facilitate shared meanings and shared realities (Smircich, 1983). First, the generation of meaning is vital not only to organizational flourishing or transcendence but also to the creation of unique value. Second, the role of a chief executive officer as the custodian of the values of the organization can be investigated to understand how changes in symbolic roles affect value creation. As Pratt and Rafaeill (1997) found, organizational symbols, such as organizational dress, for example, reveal complex social identities with multiple layers of meaning. The behaviors that make the CEO a powerful system can yield insight that illuminates our understanding of strategic roles. Third, the symbolic aspects of strategic followership can be examined given the integral link between followership and organizations. In fact, it might be important to determine the degree to which organizational symbols drive followers to behave restoratively and transcendently. As forms of identification, symbols conjure within followers a sense of ownership that compels them to act when the organization is being harmed in the form of value diminishment. However, given that symbols are sometimes vacuous, as in the phrase "merely symbolic," the strategic behavior of followers can be investigated to determine its vacuity or substantiveness.

50   *Strategic Situations*

3.2.5 Institutions

Organizations gain advantages through their regulatory behaviors. The diverse perspectives of institutions show various ways by which constraints are imposed on the interactive exchanges of individuals, groups, and organizations (Scott, 2014). According to North (1990) institutions are the 'rules of the game' and specify normative constraints on actors within a particular context. In his review of the literature on institutions across the social sciences, Scott (2014) discuss the various ways in which institutions have played a strategic role in the outcomes of not only organizations but also nations, communities, groups, and individuals. In other words, it "affects the structure and functioning of organizations" (Scott, 2014: 113). The strategic role manifests in the diverse modes of institutional carriers—relational structures, activities, and artifacts—as well as levels and variety of social, political, economic, technological elements.

In sum, the preceding theories can be used in the study of strategic situations. However, the orientation is static. Given that situations are dynamic (Mischel, 1977), it is important to consider changes of situations. The literature shows that followership is dynamic (see Uhl-Bien, Riggio, Lowe, & Carsten, 2014). Theories that facilitate studies of situational dynamics can therefore advance the science of strategic followership.

3.3 Strategic Followership Dynamics

The fundamental principle underlying strategic followership is change. The strategic situations which trigger strategic decisions and behaviors are characterized by multiple options that involve choices and potential reversion to forsaken options. In addition, followers' decisions and actions change when their supervisors (i.e., leaders) alter their behaviors or plans. For example, a leader who committed to a particular action may change course, which may, in turn, induce the follower to change course. The third source of change is the relationship itself. Relationships change, which also cause cognitive and behavioral changes in followers. It is therefore important for a strategic follower not only to know the structure of the relationship with the leader but also the relational dynamics.

Strategic followership dynamics focus on changes in the relationship which affect the value created by a follower. It refers to changes in the decisions, behaviors, and value creation of followers as a result of shifts in the decisions and behaviors of relational actors and relational contexts. Theoretical lenses for the study of strategic followership dynamics includes relational dynamics theory, social construction theory, theory of structuration, and social systems theory. While the first two have been studied at both macro and micro levels, the latter two tend to be

Strategic Situations 51

exclusively at the macro level. The focus here is on the strategic aspects of the theories. It must be noted that the four theories are interlinked in subtle ways as I discuss in the following.

3.3.1 Relational Dynamics theory

Leadership is relational; it involves a leader influencing a follower to act in a particular way (Stogdill, Goode, & Day, 1962). The term *relational*, which means "an individual likes people and thrives on relationships" (Lipman-Blumen, 1996: 165), fits with leadership research that examines relationship-oriented behavioral styles, such as consideration and supportiveness (Likert, 1961; Stogdill & Coons, 1957), or leadership behaviors that center on developing high-quality, trusting work relationships (Graen & Uhl-Bien, 1995; Uhl-Bien, Graen, & Scandura, 2000). Of course, influence does not depend on only behavior. Consequently, *relational leadership* is a recent term (Uhl-Bien, 2005, 2005) that regards knowledge as socially constructed and socially distributed, not as "mind stuff" constructed or accumulated and stored by individuals: "That which is understood as real is differently constructed in different relational and historical/cultural settings" (Dachler & Hosking, 1995: 4). Applied to leadership a relational orientation focuses on the social construction processes by which certain understandings of leadership come about and are given privileged basis (Dachler & Hosking, 1995). Uhl-Bien (2005) suggests that relational leadership involves two perspectives—entity and relational—both of which center on social processes. The entity perspective "views relational processes as centered in individuals' perceptions and cognitions as they engage in exchanges and influence relationships with one another," while the relational perspective views persons and organizations as ongoing multiple constructions made "in" processes and not the makers "of" processes (Hosking, 2000)." Uhl-Bien (2005) suggests that relational leadership is "a social influence process through which emergent coordination (i.e., evolving social order) and change (e.g., new values, attitudes, approaches, behaviors, and ideologies) are constructed and produced." According to her, leadership occurs in relational dynamics throughout the organization and as a function of the context, resulting in relational dynamics. She, however, defines relational dynamics differently because she says "the objective of Relational Leadership Theory is to enhance our understanding of the relational dynamics—the social processes—that comprise leadership and organizing" (Uhl-Bien, 2005: 666). She views relational dynamics as "a process of structuring" (p. 670).

The configurational view of Uhl-Bien and colleagues differs from the *disturbance view* of relational dynamics adopted in strategic followership. By disturbance, I mean disorientations or shifts in the relational social order that induce in followers a response. According to the

52 Strategic Situations

configurational view relational dynamics may occur without shifts and/ or any shifts are accidental and incorporated in the structuring process. However, in the disturbance view, shifts are integral and necessary; they induce a behavioral response of followers. The difference may be viewed from the actors: Configuration is leader-centered structures while disturbance is follower-centered responses. The latter may involve restructuring but that structuring is reactive rather than proactive as suggested in the configurational perspective. It fits more with the generally understood meaning of dynamic as change.

In the strategy domain of management—interorganizational relationships, buyer–supplier relationships, strategic alliances—relational dynamics refers to responses of focal or partner actors to alterations that result from either the cognitions, attitudes, or behaviors of one party or the other or the consequences associated with such responses. It is this strategic perspective that I adopt in this chapter. At the organizational (and interpersonal) level, leading and following organizations attempt to influence each other to gain competitive advantage and that influence may be in response to shifts in the cognitions and behaviors of the organizations.

Dynamics have many forms. Dooley and van de Van (1999) identify periodic, chaotic and pink noise patterns of dynamics. While periodic patterns are predictable stage-oriented changes actors encounter, chaotic patterns are unpredictable changes organizations encounter. Pink noise patterns are part of the noise (randomness) phenomena and manifest through power law relationships. They are fractal and display complex behavior (Dooley & Van de Ven, 1999). Using environmental features—state (e.g., knowledge) versus process (e.g., development), and situational features—unitary versus multiple, Zoogah (2014) identifies four types of dynamics: stage, conditional, stochastic, and network. Stage dynamics, which focus on a particular stage, result from the combination of a state attribute of either a leader or follower and a single strategic situation. For example, the incompetence of the leader on the value creation potential of the relationship is likely to vary at different levels of a leverage situation (i.e., one in which the follower has the strength to take advantage of an opportunity). *Conditional dynamics* focus on a state attribute given multiple situations. One state attribute (e.g., incompetence) that is examined over several situations (friendly, hostile, lukewarm, aggressive, constructive, etc.) is likely to show a pattern that identifies different conditions in which the relationship between the bad leadership, for example, and relationship effectiveness differ. The cross-situational specificity principle in personality psychology (Mischel, 1968) is based on this type of dynamic. Conditional dynamics take "*if . . . then . . .*" forms; they show that under one condition, (If A), the relationship between the restorative behavior and value creation is in a certain form (*then, X*), and under another condition (If B), the relationship is in another form (*then, Y*). The X–Y relationship is repeated through multiple situations but within a specific time frame. As a result, it heightens the effect of the situational attribute (Zoogah, 2014). Stochastic dynamics deal with chaos. Interactionism suggests that organizational characteristics, for example, are either static or chaotic (Chiu, Hong, & Dweck, 1997; McAdams, 1994). Chaotic dynamics is characterized by the intersection of dynamic personal attributes (leader personality, gender, experience, knowledge) and a singular situation. The variation of the changes seems unpredictable and unstable. The fourth type of dynamic involves networks. Network theory focuses on relationships among units or actors (Brass, Galaskiewicz, Greve, & Tsai, 2004). Networks are defined as systems of interrelated units, factors, events, people, and structures (Wasserman & Faust, 1994). Their level of complexity increases exponentially as the number of dimensions increases.

Leader–follower interactions sometimes take one or more of these forms of relational dynamics. Zoogah (2016) found that psychological ownership and self-monitoring attributes interacted to influence the strategic decisions of followers toward bad leaders. Studies of multiple situations and multiple attributes of both followers and leaders across multiple times are likely to show the complexity of the relational dynamics. Faems, Janssens, Madhok, and Looy (2008: 1053) examine two sequential alliances between the same firms and show

> (1) how contracts with a similar degree but different nature of formalization (narrow versus broad) trigger different kinds of trust dynamics (negative versus positive) at both operational and managerial levels, (2) how trust dynamics and contract application (rigid versus flexible) coevolve over time, and (3) how relational dynamics in previous transactions influence the design of contracts in subsequent transactions.

As equals the alliance partners might be considered leading and following firms.

Even though studies of relational dynamics from a strategic followership perspective are nonexistent, insights from the relationship-based studies at the micro level, which are termed entity-based and focus on leadership (Uhl-Bien, 2005), suggest that leadership is a "two-way influence relationship between a leader and a follower aimed primarily at attaining mutual goals" (Uhl-Bien, 2006, p. 656). The focus has been on the interpersonal relationship, most often among leader—member dyads (Uhl-Bien et al., 2000), as well as group leadership (Offstein, Madhavan, & Gnyawali, 2006). A relationship is traditionally defined as a particular type of connection existing between people related to or having dealings with each other (American Heritage Dictionary, 2000). The relational processes that are relative to individual characteristics that leaders and followers bring to their interpersonal transactions (Uhl-Bien, 2005) change depending on the psychological or nominal situation. The

54 *Strategic Situations*

relational dynamics that arise from the relational process can be examined with a focus on strategic situations.

3.3.2 Social Construction theory

Another theoretical lens for strategic followership dynamics is social construction theory (Berger & Luckmann, 1967; Burr, 2003; Gergen, 2002). It has been applied in the leadership literature because leadership is embedded in context—the person and the context are interlinked social constructions made in ongoing local, cultural, and historical processes (Dachler, 1988; Dachler & Hosking, 1995). In their review of the followership literature, Uhl-Bien et al. (2014) suggest that

> follower-centric approaches arose in response to leader-centric views and drew attention to the role of the follower in constructing leaders and leadership. They view leadership as a social construction, and leader emergence as generated in the cognitive, attributional, and social identity processes of followers.
>
> (p. 86)

The theory suggests that identities of strategic followers (and leaders) shift (and are shaped) over time as they engage in mutual influence processing (Uhl-Bien, 2005). The states of leaders and strategic followers suggest that different types of constructions of followers and leaders are likely to occur. The 'darkness' of bad leaders suggests that followers' view of leaders may be negative. Bad leaders who are not able to influence followers to adopt their negatively deviant behavior may also view the followers negatively. However, in good leadership contexts where value enhancement occurs (Zoogah, 2014), the constructions are likely to be positive. The constructions may take the form of a stable hierarchical role relationship or a shifting followership structure. The latter involves a "dynamic exchange of leadership and followership that is constantly being renegotiated across time and situations . . . [such that] the boundaries between leader and follower identities are permeable" (DeRue & Ashford, 2010: 635).

Social construction theory is also examined by strategy scholars (Mintzberg, Ahlstrand, & Lampel, 1998). The interest in interpretation or construction of what is inside the mind of executives is supposedly decoded by cognitive maps, interacts with cognition and is shaped by it. The mind enables interpretation of the environment—its malevolence or beneficence. Strategic followers' interpretation of the relational or social environment enables them to decode not only *why* but also *when* and *how* to restore diminished value. It also enables the follower to determine the likelihood of the 'bad leader' appreciating (i.e., not imposing strong consequences) the followers' actions. The ability to distinguish maleficent environments

Strategic Situations 55

from beneficent ones is a function of frames (Bateson, 1955). A cognitive or psychological frame, which is generally more complex and with different levels of interpretation, "resolves the ambiguity of what is 'inside' and what is 'outside,' what is 'real' within the context of interaction between viewer and situation and what is not" (Mintzberg et al., 1998). Psychological frames have the following properties: (a) exclusivity (including certain messages or meaningful actions while avoiding others within a frame), (b) inclusivity (excluding certain messages while certain others are included), (c) premise (tells the actor how to link the externalities to the internalities), and (d) metacommunication (the frame explicitly or implicitly provides) instructions or aids for understanding the messages included within the frame (Bateson, 1972; Mintzberg et al., 1998). Either one or all of these properties enable strategic followers not only to understand the meaning of messages from the interaction, task, social, and organizational environments but also to gauge likelihood outcomes and their potential impact. In El Sawy and Pauchant's (1988) study of how professionals and managers working as a group dealt with information about strategic opportunities in the emerging cellular telephone market shows the significance of "interaction between the initial frames and the subsequent information" (Mintzberg et al., 1998: p. 167). The interaction facilitated persuasion of group members who were hesitant to support the cellular phone frame on the dangers of the application.

Related to cognitive frames is the concept of schemas. It was initially suggested that a schema belongs to the individual (depends on what the individual sees and believes) and a frame belongs to the group (depends on group dynamics—on the relationships of individuals to each other and to the group) (Uhl-Bien, 2006). Extant research, however, shows that schemas exist in groups. Individual mental models, individual schemas, aggregate to the group level as group schemas or group mental models. Both frames and schemas constitute the cognitive school of strategy but from different perspectives with regard to the environment (Mintzberg et al., 1998). Those views and orientations toward the environment have resulted in the *objective environment*—an 'organization' is embedded within an 'environment' that has an external and independent existence (Mintzberg et al., 1998); *perceived environment*—the conception of environment (which remains real, material, and external) as a result of the incomplete and imperfect perceptions of the "environment" because of the bounded rationality of humans; and *enacted environment*—the environment is generated by human actions and accompanying intellectual efforts to make sense out of their actions.

Strategic followers may experience all three. The objective environment is the organizational context with defined authority structures that specify the relational or interaction roles. Embedded in it is how the follower conceives of the leader's attitudes and behaviors and his or her incomplete and imperfect perceptions of the relational environment. The

56 *Strategic Situations*

cognitive limitation of both the follower (and leader) affects and shapes the perceived environment. The latter environment thus determines how the strategic follower enacts and makes sense of both his or her actions vis-à-vis those of the leader and the effects on the organization or relational constituents. How well the strategic follower interprets the events, objects, and situations of the relationship determines the meaningfulness of his or her decisions and actions.

In sum, social constructionism acts as an epistemological standpoint and assumes that a strategic follower's reality is actively created by and in social relationships and interactions with leaders. Thus, the follower's knowledge is not a definitive depiction of what exists independently of him or her but is socially constructed (Uhl-Bien, 2005). The social constructionist view suggests that followers' relational environment may be error-laden for three reasons. First, because of bounded rationality, followers may not have all essential stimuli or information to optimize on their interpretations or decisions. Second, the cognitive constraint will limit their interpretation competence; while one follower may derive one meaning from the actions of a leader (e.g., value-diminishing behavior), another may derive another meaning (value-enhancing behavior). This difference is exacerbated by the strategic situation, which presents multiple options. Third, the relational environment changes, which means the sense of objectivity, perception, and enactment, are also likely to change.

3.3.3 *Theory of Structuration*

Structuration theory asserts that organizations are avenues of regular interaction between members and the repeated interactions facilitate social order (Dachler & Hosking, 1995; Hatch, 1997). Although the repetitive interactions might suggest the organization is strong and its formal managerial leaders are "in charge" of events that occur around them (Sjöstrand, Sandberg, & Tyrstrup, 2001; Streatfield, 2001), structuration theory indicates that in reality, structures are highly dynamic and open to several minute changes because of their dependence on the daily reproduction of the interaction patterns that constitute them: "If interaction patterns are disrupted or changed, then the social structure is opened to change" (Hatch, 1997: 180). One function of leadership is the creation of change in organizations (Bryman, 1996). Thus, structuring occurs through the managerial role and the "disruptions" of daily interaction patterns that effect change in structure. The changes may be unwitting or intentional, proactive or reactive, strategic or nonstrategic for both leader and follower (Uhl-Bien, Marion, & McKelvey, 2004).

Hosking (1988) suggests that order is negotiated through a process of decision-making in which one or more participants may decide that the status quo "is changing, is likely to change, or is in need of change, and takes action on that basis" (p. 156). That participant may be a strategic

Strategic Situations 57

follower. When this occurs, the follower interprets actual and potential events in relation to values and interests and in relation to beliefs about causal connections (i.e., relationships and networks) within the dyad, department, or organization (Hosking, 1988). As strategic followers make decisions about whether and how to approach changes to the status quo, their previously established social relations or social capital becomes important (Uhl-Bien, 2005). Networking or social capital here refers to a major organizing activity, one that makes a difference in understanding of the role of the status quo and response to it in such a way that defends or uplifts values and interests (Uhl-Bien, 2005). It is very important for strategic followers because of their tendency to create value through restorative or transcendent behaviors. Networking helps them to "(a) build up their knowledge bases and other resources; (b) come to understand the processes through which they can promote their values and interests, and (c) translate their understandings into action" (Hosking, 1988: 158–159). For restorative followers, networking may help them mobilize social resources for restoration. The same with transcendent followers: Networking helps them persuade a leader to optimize value creation. Structuration theory can thus be used to understand not only changes in relational structures but also in the mobilization of resources to adjust to the changes.

The theory of structuration does not emphasize the reality construction process that occurs between the follower and the leader actors or the interactions between them. Rather, it is the social practices that persist over time and space (Giddens, 1984). According to Giddens (1984), social practices are important because they represent a mode of connection between action theory (here based on social constructionism) and structural analysis. According to the theory the leader–follower exchange, as practices, exist as regularized activities of followers and leaders that bring about relations of interdependence between them and their organizations. The exchange is a social practice, a routinized type of behavior of the followers and leaders as individuals or organizations (Giddens, 1979: 66). Followers can make a difference in the strategy processes (i.e., contribution to the strategic objectives of the organization), and it encourages a review of interpretations and experiences not only of leaders but also those of followers. Thus, followers are not framed as all-powerful actors who are fearless but as skilled, knowledgeable, and intentional agents desirous of effecting a positive change in organizations (Zoogah, 2014). Agency "does not refer to a series of discrete and combined acts, but to a continuous flow of conduct" (Giddens, 1979: 55). Follower agency is therefore more than a function of individual behavior; it means having choice and effecting decisions even though the outcome might lead to unintended consequences. According to Giddens (1979), follower agency and the 'strategizing' that undergirds it can be explained "as practical-evaluative agency" (Jarzabkowski, 2005: 30).

58 *Strategic Situations*

Gidden's theory is mainly based on examining the habitual actions of individuals, actions that individuals engage in without deliberate thought. Such routinized behavior, in turn, depends on the rationalization of followers' actions, which can be understood as a mix of process and capability on the part of the followers. It thus becomes possible to examine applied strategy (e.g., to analyze post-rationalized actions as found in narrated stories of followers or observations of applied strategies of followers). The dynamics of routines can thus be applied to strategic followership.

3.3.4 Social Systems theory

Another theoretical lens for examining relational dynamics of strategic followership is social systems theory. Organizations are complex social systems (Katz & Kahn, 1978). The social system theory (Luhmann, 2000) therefore provides a broad background of insights and concepts that are useful when studying complex interaction systems (Baecker, 2003; Nicolai, 2000). In dyadic interactions, the relationships are fairly simple and therefore less susceptible to social systems theoretical propositions. However, in multilateral followership relationships (see Uhl-Bien et al., 2014), the systems are complex and can be understood through the social systems theoretical lens. In accordance with social system theory, a following organization will expand its decision-making scope by developing processes for self-observation and self-description. Value creation that is for the future benefit of the relational constituents manifests itself in activities related not only to perceiving, observing, and interpreting but also to building an environment that is conducive to relationships and interaction.

According to this perspective, strategy as a whole, or its subcomponents (e.g., strategic decisions), are tied to the follower's communication network. Strategies are patterned connectivities between leader–follower exchange events (communications, actions, decisions) for sustaining the strategic follower in the long term. Consequently, the strategic follower orients him- or herself based on a clearly defined strategic framework. Developing alternate courses of action is thus a prerequisite for successfully coping with the complex exchange between a bad leader and a strategic follower. This reasoning underlies Zoogah's (2014) assertion that strategic followership involves a high level of generativity.

3.4 Other Theoretical Lenses

In addition to the preceding theoretical lenses, theories of strategic context (Gupta & Govindarajan, 1991) can also be used to examine the relational dynamics of strategic followership. Gupta and Govindarajan (1991) suggest that there are differences in strategic contexts. In the case of multinational corporations, the Multinational Corporation (MNC) can be modeled as a network of transactions which shows the "specific ways in which strategic contexts of various subsidiaries can differ" (p. 771). They use the magnitude of transactions (the volume and criticality of intracorporate transactions) and directionality of transactions (whether they are either the receivers or the providers of what is being transacted) to identify four types of strategic contexts—global innovator, local innovator, integrated player, and implementer—for subsidiary transactions. A following firm can be a global innovator when there is high outflow and low inflow of knowledge between the relational partners. A local innovation is characterized by low outflow and inflow of knowledge between the partners. Implementer firms have low outflow of knowledge but high inflow of knowledge from relational partners. Last, integrated players are characterized by high outflow and inflow of knowledge. These contexts vary and consequently change as a function of time and environment. For strategic followership at the firm level, these contexts can be used to examine the relational dynamics of following and leading firm exchanges.

Furthermore, the prototypic internal (strengths and weakness) and external (opportunities and threats) environmental dimensions, four strategic contexts—leverage, vulnerability, constraint, and problem—define not only the patterns of relating between firms (Hardy & Phillips, 1998) but also the influence dynamics. In leverage contexts, the follower is strong (as defined by experience, competence, knowledge, attitude, etc., that is superior) to take advantage of opportunity in the relational environment external to the parties. That capability differs from one in which the follower is strong but faces threats from the external environment. The vulnerability of the follower represents a different capability context. The third context, strategic constraint, is characterized by weakness and opportunity; even though there is opportunity in the external environment, the follower is weak and therefore is constrained from exploiting the opportunities. Last, in problematic contexts, followers are weak and yet face threats from the external environment. The combined limitations of weakness and threats undermine the ability of the follower to achieve any strategic outcomes. These theories function at the firm level. However, they can be applied at the individual level. Zoogah (2010) used the internal and external relational environments to identify contexts similar to those that apply at the interpersonal or individual level.

Fiske's (1993) relational contexts have been studied at the interpersonal level. Each relational context is distinct in the rules and values of how the people interact—communal-sharing, authority-ranking, equality-matching, and market-pricing relationships. In communal-sharing relationships, people exist together in a trusting relationship whereby they share many things, considering them as 'ours' rather than 'mine.' Fairness is important in such groups, and appealing to values may be the best

60 *Strategic Situations*

way to persuade members. Conflict is often dealt with through mediation and other methods that seek agreement from all. Examples include kinship relationships. In authority-ranking relationships such as social groups and organizations there is a hierarchy of power and defined lines of reporting. They are similar to command and control structures where the inferior person has little option but to obey the superior person. In equality-matching relationships there are no authority ranks between people, nor is there the deeper responsibility toward one another as in the communal-sharing model. Equality-matched relationships are generally based on collaboration around shared goals and helping one another on the basis of appeals and a loose exchange of favors. Last, in market-pricing relationships, the relational exchange is based around a transaction, where the parties exchange substantive items, often with money being a part of the transaction.

However, they can be applied at the firm level. Interfirm relationships are characterized by the equality matching and market pricing. First, there is no authority between the firms but there is collaboration around shared goals and help to one another on the basis of appeals or a loose exchange of favors. In addition to this equality-matching attribute, the relationship may be based on a specific transaction where substantive items are exchanged between the firms. While leverage and vulnerability situations may be associated with equality-matching patterns, constraint and problem situations might be associated with market-pricing relationships. The influence dynamics in equality matching is based on appeals or loose exchanges while that of the market pricing is based on transactions or hard exchanges (Fiske, 1993). The strategic context thus affects the strategic interactions of a following and leading firms.

To conclude theories that fit with the environment (strategic situations and dynamics) can be used to investigate the third component of strategic followership. Some theories focus on micro or interpersonal relations while others focus on the interorganizational relations. I also discuss theories on the dynamics of strategic followership. Zoogah (2014) draws from the triad of followership—leader, follower, and situation—to propose strategic situations as a central element of strategic followership. The theory of strategic followership centers on contexts—strategic situation, bad leadership context, and good leadership context. In the latter two, strategic followers enact restorative and transcendent followership roles, respectively. The decisions undergirding those role enactments depend on the strategic situations followers encounter. It is important to note that game theory provides a rigorous approach to modeling what rational actors behaving with self-interest are likely to do in well-defined situations—provision of valuable insights when situations permit simple questions—but it does not necessarily provide yes or no answers to questions centered on whether it is wise to balance the power of dominant relational constituents (Mintzberg et al., 1998). In that regard, it is descriptive.

References

Alchian, A. A. (1950). Uncertainty, evolution, and economic theory. *Journal of political economy*, 58(3), 211–221.

Baecker, R. (2003). A principled design for scalable internet visual communications with rich media, interactivity, and structured archives. Paper Presented at the Proceedings of the 2003 Conference of the Centre for Advanced Studies on Collaborative research IBM Press, Toronto, Ontario, Canada, (pp. 16–29).

Baer, M., Dirks, K. T., & Nickerson, J. A. (2012). Microfoundations of strategic problem formulation. *Strategic Management Journal*, 2(34), 197–214.

Baer, M., Dirks, K. T., & Nickerson, J. A. (2013). Microfoundations of strategic problem formulation. *Strategic Management Journal*, 34(2), 197–214.

Barney, J. (1991). Firm resources and sustained competitive advantage. *Journal of Management*, 17(1), 99–120.

Bateson, G. (1955). A theory of play and fantasy; A report on theoretical aspects of the project of study of the role of the paradoxes of abstraction in communication. *Psychiatric Research Reports*, 2, 39–51.

Bateson, G. (1972). The logical categories of learning and communication. Steps to an Ecology of Mind, 279–308.

Becker, M. C. (2004). Organizational routines: A review of the literature. *Industrial and corporate change*, 13(4), 643–678.

Berg, P. O. (1986). Symbolic management of human resources. *Human Resource Management*, 25(4), 557–579.

Berger, P., & Luckmann, T. (1967). *The Social Construction of Reality*. London: Allen Lane. Google Scholar.

Brass, D. J., Galaskiewicz, J., Greve, H. R., & Tsai, W. (2004). Taking stock of networks and organizations: A multilevel perspective. *Academy of Management Journal*, 47(6), 795–817.

Bryman, A. (1996). *Social Science Research*. Oxford: Oxford University Press.

Burr, V. (2003). *Social Constructionism*. London: Routledge.

Child, J. (1972). Organizational structure, environment and performance: The role of strategic choice. *Sociology*, 6(1), 1–22.

Child, J. (1975). Managerial and organizational factors associated with company performance-part II. A contingency analysis. *Journal of Management Studies*, 12(1–2), 12–27.

Chiu, C. Y., Hong, Y. Y., & Dweck, C. S. (1997). Lay dispositionism and implicit theories of personality. *Journal of Personality and Social Psychology*, 73(1), 19.

Cohen, M. D., & Bacdayan, P. (1994). Organizational routines are stored as procedural memory: Evidence from a laboratory study. *Organization Science*, 5(4), 554–568.

Coman, A., & Ronen, B. (2007). Managing strategic and tactical constraints in the hi-tech industry. *International Journal of Production Research*, 45(4), 779–788.

Courpasson, D., & Dany, F. (2003). Indifference or obedience? Business firms as democratic hybrids. *Organization Studies*, 24(8), 1231–1260.

Cowan, D. A. (1986). Developing a process model of problem recognition. *Academy of Management Review*, 11(4), 763–776.

Dachler, H. P. (1988). Constraints on the emergence of new vistas in leadership and management research: An epistemological overview. Emerging Leadership Vistas, 261–285.

62 Strategic Situations

Dachler, H. P., & Hosking, D. M. (1995). *The primacy of relations in socially constructing organizational realities* (PhD dissertation).

Dandrige, T. C., Mitroff, I., & Joyce, W. F. (1980). Organizational symbolism: A topic to expand organizational analysis. *Academy of Management Review*, 5(1), 77–82.

DeRue, D. S., & Ashford, S. J. (2010). Who will lead and who will follow? A social process of leadership identity construction in organizations. *Academy of Management Review*, 35(4), 627–647.

Dictionary, A. H. (2000). The American Heritage® Dictionary of the English Language. Answers.com.

Dooley, K. J., & Van de Ven, A. H. (1999). Explaining complex organizational dynamics. *Organization Science*, 10(3), 358–372.

Dosi, G., Faillo, M., & Marengo, L. 2008. Organizational Capabilities, Patterns of Knowledge Accumulation and Governance Structures in Business Firms: An Introduction. *Organization Studies*, 29, 1165–1185.

El Sawy, O. A., & Pauchant, T. C. (1988). Triggers, templates and twitches in the tracking of emerging strategic issues. *Strategic Management Journal*, 9(5), 455–473.

Faems, D., Janssens, M., Madhok, A., & Looy, B. V. (2008). Toward an integrative perspective on alliance governance: Connecting contract design, trust dynamics, and contract application. *Academy of Management Journal*, 51(6), 1053–1078.

Feldman, M. S., & Pentland, B. T. (2003). Reconceptualizing organizational routines as a source of flexibility and change. *Administrative Science Quarterly*, 48(1), 94–118.

Felin, T., & Foss, N. J. (2009). Organizational routines and capabilities: Historical drift and a course-correction toward micro-foundations. *Scandinavian Journal of Management*, 25(2), 157–167.

Fiske, S. T. (1993). Social cognition and social perception. *Annual Review of Psychology*, 44(1), 155–194.

Gergen, K. J. (2002). Social construction and practical theology. The dance begins. *Social Constructionism and Theology*, 3–21.

Giddens, A. (1979). Agency, structure. In *Central Problems in Social Theory* (pp. 49–95). London: Palgrave Macmillan.

Giddens, A. (1984). *The Construction of Society*. Cambridge: Polity.

Glauser, M. J. (1984). Upward information flow in organizations: Review and conceptual analysis. *Human Relations*, 37(8), 613–643.

Goffman, E. (1974). *Frame Analysis: An Essay on the Organization of Experience*. Boston, MA: Harvard University Press.

Graen, G. B., & Uhl-Bien, M. (1995). Relationship-based approach to leadership: Development of leader-member exchange (LMX) theory of leadership over 25 years: Applying a multi-level multi-domain perspective. *The Leadership Quarterly*, 6(2), 219–247.

Gupta, A. K., & Govindarajan, V. (1991). Knowledge flows and the structure of control within multinational corporations. *Academy of Management Review*, 16(4), 768–792.

Hardy, C., & Phillips, N. (1998). Strategies of engagement: Lessons from the critical examination of collaboration and conflict in an interorganizational domain. *Organization Science*, 9(2), 217–230.

Hatch, M. J. (1997). Irony and the social construction of contradiction in the humor of a management team. *Organization Science*, 8(3), 275–288.

Hosking, D. M. (1988). Organizing, leadership and skilful process. *Journal of Management Studies*, 25(2), 147–166.

Hosking, D. M. (2000). 'Ecology in mind, mindful practices', *European Journal of Work and Organizational Psychology*, 9(2): 147–158.

Hull, C. E., & Lio, B. H. (2006). Innovation in non-profit and for-profit organizations: Visionary, strategic, and financial considerations. *Journal of Change Management*, 6(1), 53–65.

Jain, A. K., & Singal, A. K. (2014). Mapping vulnerability: How emerging markets respond to multinationals. *Journal of Business Strategy*, 35(6), 41–48.

Jarzabkowski, P. (2005). *Strategy as practice: An activity-based approach*. London: Sage.

Katz, D., & Kahn, R. L. (1978). *The Social Psychology of Organizations* (Vol. 2, p. 528). New York: Wiley.

Kellerman, B. (2008). *Followership: How Followers Are Creating Change and Changing Leaders*. Boston: Harvard Business School Press

Koestler, A. (1967). *The Act of Creation: A Study of the Conscious and Unconscious in Science and Art*. New York: Dell Publishing Company.

Lele, M. M. (1992). *Creating Strategic Leverage: Matching Company Strengths with Market Opportunities*. New York: Wiley.

Likert, R. (1961). *New Patterns of Management*. New York: McGraw – Hill.

Lipman-Blumen, J. (1996). *The Connective Edge: Leading in an Interdependent World*. San Francisco, CA: Jossey-Bass.

Lipparini, A., & Sobrero, M. (1994). The glue and the pieces: Entrepreneurship and innovation in small-firm networks. *Journal of Business Venturing*, 9(2), 125–140.

Luhmann, N. (2000). *Art as a Social System*. Stanford, CA: Stanford University Press.

Lyles, M. A., & Mitroff, I. I. (1980). Organizational problem formulation: An empirical study. *Administrative Science Quarterly*, 102–119.

Matsa, D. A. (2010). Capital structure as a strategic variable: Evidence from collective bargaining. *The Journal of Finance*, 65(3), 1197–1232.

McAdams, D. P. (1994). Can personality change? Levels of stability and growth in personality across the life span. In Heatherton, T. F. & Weinberger, J. L. (Eds.), *Can Personality Change?* (pp. 299–313). Washington, DC: American Psychological Association.

Mead, G. H. (1934). *Mind, Self and Society* (Vol. 111). Chicago: University of Chicago Press.

Milliken, F. J., Morrison, E. W., & Hewlin, P. F. (2003). An exploratory study of employee silence: Issues that employees don't communicate upward and why. *Journal of Management Studies*, 40(6), 1453–1476.

Mintzberg, H., Ahlstrand, B., & Lampel, J. (1998). *Strategy Safari: A Guided Tour Through the Wilds of Strategic Management*. New York: Free Press.

Mischel, W. (1968). *Personality and Assessment*. New York: Wiley.

Mischel, W. 1977. The interaction of person and situation. In Magnusson, D. & Endler, N. S. (Eds.), *Personality at the Crossroads: Current Issues in Interactional Psychology* (pp. 333–352). Hillsdale, NJ: Earlbaum.

64 Strategic Situations

Mischel, W., & Shoda, Y. (2010). The situated person. *The Mind in Context*, 149–173.

Myerson, R. B. (1993). Effectiveness of electoral systems for reducing government corruption: a game-theoretic analysis. *Games and Economic Behavior*, 5, 118–132.

Navare, S. (2008). Counselling at work place: A proactive human resource initiative. *Indian Journal of Occupational and Environmental Medicine*, 12(1), 1–2.

Nelson, R. R., & Winter, S. G. (1982). The Schumpeterian tradeoff revisited. *The American Economic Review*, 72(1), 114–132.

Newell, A., & Simon, H. A. (1972). Human Problem Solving (Vol. 104, No. 9). Englewood Cliffs, NJ: Prentice Hall.

Nicolai, W. (2000). U.S. Patent No. 6,155,660. Washington, DC: U.S. Patent and Trademark Office.

North, D. C. (1990). A transaction cost theory of politics. *Journal of theoretical politics*, 2(4), 355–367.

Offstein, E. H., Madhavan, R., & Gnyawali, D. R. (2006). Pushing the frontier of LMX research. *Sharing Network Leadership*, 4, 95.

Oliver, C. (1991). Strategic responses to institutional processes. *Academy of Management Review*, 16(1), 145–179.

Parmigiani, A., & Howard-Grenville, J. (2011). Routines revisited: Exploring the capabilities and practice perspectives. *Academy of Management Annals*, 5(1), 413–453.

Pentland, B. T., & Feldman, M. (2005). Organizationalroutines as a unit of analysis. *Industrial and Corporate Change*, 14(5), 793–815.

Pentland, B. T., & Rueter, H. (1994). Organizational routines as grammars of action. *Administrative Science Quarterly*, 39, 484–510.

Pratt, M. G. & Rafaelli, A. (1997). Organizational dress as a symbol of multi-layered social identities. *Academy of Management Journal*, 40(4), 862–898.

Ross, J. M., & Sharapov, D. (2015). When the leader follows: Avoiding dethronement through imitation. *Academy of Management Journal*, 58(3), 658–679.

Rousseau, D. M., & Fried, Y. (2001). Location, location, location: Contextualizing organizational research. *Journal of Organizational Behavior: The International Journal of Industrial, Occupational and Organizational Psychology and Behavior*, 22(1), 1–13.

Schumpeter, J.A. (1934), *Change and the Entrepreneur*. Cambridge, MA: Harvard University Press.

Schwartz, S. H. (1992). Universals in the content and structure of values: Theoretical advances and empirical tests in 20 countries. In Zanna, M. P. (Ed.), *Advances in Experimental Social Psychology* (Vol. 25, pp. 1–65). New York: Academic Press.

Scott, W. R. (2014). *Institutions and Organizations* (4th ed.). London, UK: Sage Publication.

Smircich, L. (1983). Concepts of culture and organizational analysis. *Administrative Science Quarterly*, 28, 339–358.

Sjöstrand, S. E., Sandberg, J., & Tyrstrup, M. (2001). *Invisible Management: The Social Construction of Leadership*. London: Thomson Learning.

Spector, Y. (2011). Theory of constraint methodology where the constraint is the business model. *International Journal of Production Research*, 49(11), 3387–3394.

Spekman, R. E. (1988). Strategic supplier selection: Understanding long-term buyer relationships. *Business Horizons*, 31(4), 75–81.

Stogdill, R. M., & Coons, A. E. (1957). *Leader Behavior: Its Description and Measurement*. Columbos, Ohio: Ohio State University Press for Bureau of Business Research.

Stogdill, R. M., Goode, O. S., & Day, D. R. (1962). New leader behavior description subscales. *The Journal of Psychology*, 54(2), 259–269.

Streatfield, P. (2001). *The Paradox of Control in Organizations*. London: Routledge.

Tynan, R. (2005). The effects of threat sensitivity and face giving on dyadic psychological safety and upward communication 1. *Journal of Applied Social Psychology*, 35(2), 223–247.

Uhl-Bien, M. (2005). Implicit theories of relationships in the workplace. In Schyns, B. & Meindl, J. (Eds.), *Implicit Leadership Theories: Essays and Explorations* (pp. 103–133). Greenwich, CT: Information Age Publishing.

Uhl-Bien, M., Graen, G. B., & Scandura, T. A. (2000). Implications of leader-member exchange (LMX) for strategic human resource management systems: Relationships as social capital for competitive advantage. *Research in Personnel and Human Resources Management*, 18, 137–186.

Uhl-Bien, M., Marion, R., & McKelvey, B. (2004). Complexity leadership theory: Shifting leadership from the industrial age to the knowledge era. Paper Presented at the National Academy of Management Meeting, New Orleans, LA.

Uhl-Bien, M., Riggio, R. E., Lowe, K. B., & Carsten, M. K. (2014). Followership theory: A review and research agenda. *The Leadership Quarterly*, 25(1), 83–104.

Veblen, T. (1898). Why is economics not an evolutionary science? *The Quarterly Journal of Economics*, 12(4), 373–397.

Wasserman, S., & Faust, K. (1994). *Social Network Analysis: Methods and Applications* (Vol. 8). Cambridge: Cambridge University Press.

Whitehead, C. J., Blair, J. D., Smith, R. R., Nix, T. W., & Savage, G. T. (1989). Stakeholder supportive-ness and strategic vulnerability: Implications for competitive strategy in the HMO industry. *Health Care Management Review*, 14, 65–76.

Williamson, O. E. (1991). Comparative economic organization: The analysis of discrete structural alternatives. *Administrative Science Quarterly*, 269–296.

Winter, S. G. (2005). Developing evolutionary theory for economics and management. *Great Minds in Management*, 509–546.

Winter, S. G. (1964). Economic "natural selection" and the theory of the firm (Vol. 4, pp. 225–272). Institute of Business and Economic Research, University of California.

Wisner, B., Blaikie, P., Cannon, T., & Davis, I. (2004). *At Risk: Natural Hazards, People's Vulnerability and Disasters*. London: Routledge.

Zoogah, D. B. (2016). Stressful Situations and Strategic Followers' Response Behaviors. The Role of Values-based Leadership and Followership in Employee Stress Symposium. Academy of Management Annual Meeting, Anaheim, California, August 5–9, 2016.

Zoogah, D. B. (2014). Dynamic analysis and strategy in Africa. In Zoogah, D. B. (Ed.), *Advancing Research Methodology in the African Context: Techniques,*

66 Strategic Situations

Methods, and Designs (Research Methodology in Strategy and Management, Vol. 10, pp. 99–132). UK: Emerald Group Publishing.

Zoogah, D. B. (2010, April). *With You or Under You? A Multilevel Model of Virtuous Followership for Leader-Follower Relationship Effectiveness.* Society for Industrial and Organizational Psychology, Chicago, Illinois.

Zoogah, D. B. (2014). *Strategic Followership: How Followers Impact Organizational Effectiveness.* New York, NY: Palgrave Macmillan.

4 Strategic Decisions and Actions

What is the process by which followers decide to (1) restore value diminished as a result of bad leadership or (2) optimize subpar value emerging from good leadership? What actions do followers take? These are major questions that elucidate strategic followership. Followers make decisions and take actions that yield value for relational constituents. It is therefore important to explore theories that seem suitable for strategic decisions and strategic behavior of followers. Uncertainty and risk theories that underlie decision-making of organizational leaders can also be used to understand the decision-making of strategic followers. Strategic actions are behaviors that result from strategic decisions. Consequently, I discuss theoretical perspectives that center on strategic action.

4.1 Strategic Decisions

Decisions are cognitive elements. In the strategy literature, they are often regarded as part of strategic cognition. The cognitive school of strategic management shows that strategy formation is a mental process (Mintzberg, Ahlstrand, & Lampel, 1998). Both the positivistic view, which "treats the processing and structuring of knowledge as an effort to produce some kind of objective motion picture of the world," and the constructivist view, which contends that strategy is some kind of interpretation of the events, the symbols, the behavior of customer or world of the organization (Mintzberg et al., 1998: 155), suggest that cognitive bias, or the mental limitations of the strategist, information processing of managers and organizations, and how the mind maps the structures of knowledge, influence behaviors of managers and organizations in varied ways. Strategic cognition research shows that organizational strategies result from strategic consensus (the process by which organizations reach consensus on desired strategies and outcomes; Walsh, 1995), managerial cognition (the process by which cognitions of managers influence their orientation to strategic systems of organizations; Eden, Spender, & Spender, 1998), and organizational cognition (the process by which cognitive systems of organizations impact systems and operations of

68 *Strategic Decisions and Actions*

organizations; Hodgkinson & Healey, 2008; Mintzberg et al., 1998). Together they show that cognitive structures of individual managers, teams, organizations, and industries influence organizational operations (Mintzberg et al., 1998). I begin with game theory.

4.1.1 Game Theory

Discussed one aspect of game theory in the previous chapter. In this chapter, I focus on another aspect, evolutionary game theory. Economic game theory is a major lens for strategy scholars that examine not only the behaviors but also decisions of organizational actors. In the followership and leadership literature, the focus has been on evolutionary game theory. In Van Vugt's (2006) evolutionary origins of leadership and followership, "leadership is reconceptualized in terms of the outcome of strategic interactions among individuals who are following different, yet complementary, decision rules to solve recurrent coordination problems" (p. 354). He tests several evolutionary hypotheses about the origins of leadership and followership in humans and finds that "leadership correlates with initiative taking, trait measures of intelligence, specific task competencies, and several indicators of generosity" (p. 354). Given that "leadership evolved specifically for the purpose of solving coordination problems" and "individuals who frequently engage in group activities face a recurrent decision problem" (p. 359), he argues that "leadership and followership are social strategies that have been selected for by virtue of their success in fostering collective action" and uses evolutionary game theory (Maynard-Smith, 1982), sometimes referred to as "evolutionary stable strategy" (ESS), or ESS theory, to model social interactions as games in which strategies compete with each other in a Darwinian fashion. He distinguishes evolutionary game theory from economic game theory by arguing that in the former, the agents are genes that embody strategies that over the course of evolution are tested against alternative strategies and copies of themselves in terms of their relative fitness. Superior strategies that might be considered genes diffuse through a population because of the superior decision rules the actors adopt in relevant situations, whereas inferior strategies become extinct because they are jettisoned. This process is similar to natural selection (Dawkins, 1976).

Evolutionary game theory can be used to examine strategic followership by modeling leadership and followership as different strategies for social interaction that creates value. Evolutionary game theory can also be used to examine how well the dimensions of strategic followership fare against alternative strategies as well as each other. In commenting on Van Vugt's (2006) evolutionary game theory, Guastello (2008) points out that "the connections between group coordination, leadership, and game theory have some prior history (Guastello, Bock, Caldwell, & Bond,

2005; Guastello & Bond, 2007; Guastello & Guastello, 1998)" (p. 53). He notes that "contrary to conventional thinking, there is more than one type of coordination in game theory" because while the Prisoner's Dilemma game discussed in the previous chapter (see Figures 3.1–3.3), involves choices between cooperation and competition, the Stag Hunt game involves choices between joining the group (to hunt stag) and going off on one's own (to hunt rabbits), and "[t]he Intersection game requires group members to take the correct actions in the correct sequence and to figure out the correct sequence" (Guastello, 2008: 54). In the latter two games, individuals make decisions on the basis of the utilities associated with the options. One potential negative outcome of the Stag Hunt game is social loafing or the free-rider problem (Guastello, 2008). The stag hunt is a game that describes a conflict between safety and social cooperation. Other names for it or its variants include "assurance game," "coordination game," and "trust dilemma." Jean-Jacques Rousseau describes a transaction situation where two people go for a hunt.[1] Instead of animals I prefer birds. So, I call it the bird hunt game. There are some birds that are difficult to hunt, and cooperation is needed in much the same way as hunting a stag or hare. The difficulty in hunting the birds suggests birds that are more difficult to hunt are worth more than those that are easy to hunt. In the game, each person can individually choose to hunt a chukar or ptarmigan. A chukar is relatively more difficult to hunt and therefore seems to have more value than a ptarmigan. So each player must choose an action without knowing the choice of the other. If an individual hunts a chukar he or she must have the cooperation of the partner in order to succeed. An individual can get a ptarmigan by him- or herself, but a ptarmigan is worth less than a chukar. It is therefore an analogy for social cooperation such that cooperation with another person yields superior outcomes than noncooperation. An example of the payoff matrix for the bird hunt is pictured in Figure 4.1. It shows a generic (a) and more specific (b) bird hunt game.

Consistent with Friedman (1994) as well as Friedman and Sunder (1994), who points out that the majority of game theory experiments are conducted without leaders or even without talking between the

	Chukar	Ptarmigan
Chukar	2, 2	0, 1
Ptarmigan	1, 0	1, 1

Figure 4.1 The Bird Hunting Game

70   *Strategic Decisions and Actions*

participants, suggesting equality of agents or strategic actors, game theory can thus be applied to strategic followership decision-making because of the assumption of equality of the follower and the leader. The major problem with evolutionary game theory is that it is premised on a large volume of simple dyadic interactions that produce global outcomes for the social system. However, individuals may prefer hierarchical rules or strategies such as tit for tat. Van Vugt et al. (2008) suggests "the leader game" (p. 185), but Guastello (2008) points out that it is not really about leaders and followers; rather, it is better known as the War of the Sexes (Zagare, 1984) because *He* and *She* enjoy each other's company and want to do things together. It is likely *He* wants to go to a sporting event, and *She* wants to go to a horticultural exhibit, and neither is really interested in the other's choice of entertainment. The single shot has no equilibrium but attains one if there are repeated interactions in which the couple alternates entertainment choices.

4.1.2 Crisis Decision Theory

Institutional and organizational crisis theories implicate decision-making, but it is crisis decision theory that explicitly addresses the decision-making process during crisis situations. As a meta theory, crisis decision theory (Sweeney, 2008) integrates literature on coping, health behavior, and decision-making into three stages that describe the three stages of responding to negative events. The theory suggests that entities who encounter a negative event assess its severity, determine response options, and evaluate those options. The theory merges coping theories (e.g. the transactional model of stress and coping; Lazarus & Folkman, 1984) with the self-regulation model of illness (Leventhal, Meyer, & Nerenz, 1980) to predict the responses people are likely to choose when they encounter a negative event. Crisis decision theory (1) "addresses responses to negative events that have already occurred and not proactive attempts to prevent the occurrence of negative events," (2) "is not a prescriptive or evaluative theory," and (3) has a primary function of describing the "processes involved in responding to negative events and to predict response choices" (Sweeney, 2008: 62). Nevertheless, it has been applied to other crisis situations, including supply chain (Schippers, Rook, & van de Velde, 2011), adult development (Turner, Goodin, & Lokey, 2012), and leadership (Pittinsky, Hadley, & Sommer, 2009).

The crisis literature shows that crises—low-probability, high-impact events that threaten the security and well-being of individuals, groups, and organizations (Pearson & Clair, 1998)—are pressures on those entities, as pressures crises vary in intensity (Pearson & Clair, 1998) and require variation in decision activities. This approach to decision-making can therefore be used to examine bad situations, such as those involving bad leaders and strategic followers. The latter has to assess not only the severity of the leader's bad behavior and to determine his or her response options but also to evaluate the response options in terms of their feasibility, consequences, and value in the short and long term. It would seem foolhardy for a follower to take an action that yields negative outcomes. In fact, that would be contrary to strategic followership theory, which is positively valenced. In sum, the theory can be used to describe the decisions strategic followers make when their relationship with leaders (e.g., supervisors) devolve into crisis.

4.1.3 Strategic Choice Theory

In contrast to strategic response behavior, which is theorized at the organizational level but applied to the individual level, strategic choice theory is theorized at the individual level but can be applied at the organizational level (Child, 1972, 1997). It is based on the view that institutional pressures are not limited to organizations only; they can be faced by smaller groups and individuals. It describes the role that leaders play in influencing an organization through making choices in a dynamic political process. Strategic choice theory provides an alternative that emphasizes the agency of individuals and groups within organizations to make choices, sometimes serving their own ends, that dynamically influence the development of those organizations. The strategic choices form part of the entity's learning process that adapts to the external environment as well as the internal political situation. Strategic choice theory is sometimes studied with regard to individuals' responses in ordinary, everyday disputes. Keating, Pruitt, Eberle, and Mikolic (1994) examine strategic choice in everyday disputes and found that both complainants and respondents used a variety of strategies that changed over time in an effort to resolve the dispute. The theory can therefore be used to understand how followers resolve disputes with bad leaders. Keating et al.'s (1994) study, for example, can be applied to strategic followership.

An emergent strategic choice, defined as the tendency for a follower to respond to ineffectual leadership situations by explicitly deciding not to act openly against the leader but to let the response emerge from the subsequent interactions between them given the passage of time, may also be better. As the most passive, this response involves delay, excuse, and plea tactics. A follower who is unwilling to succumb to bad leadership may delay fulfillment of the leader's demand under the belief that the passage of time will change the situation. For example, a leader may change his or her mind following reflection on the demand. Delay may also be used as an indirect tactic, a signal to the leader that the follower is unwilling to explicitly succumb to the leader's demand. Excuse tactics are intended to drag out the follower's nonconformity. A follower adopting this tactic buys for time not to conform to the leader's expectations while hoping that the relationship between them

72 Strategic Decisions and Actions

will be maintained. It seems more likely to be adopted when the follower is concerned about either the consequences or the relationship. A plea refers to a follower's advocacy for nonconformity. It differs from excuses, which are subtle prevarications. With pleas, a follower explicitly requests a leader consider his or her situation (usually precarious). It is more likely to be used when the follower is afraid of the consequences of nonconformity. Other strategic choices such as those in game theory may also be investigated.

4.1.4 Information Asymmetry

Theory suggests that the pattern of information distribution between two units (i.e., individuals, groups, departments, and organizations) affects how decisions are made and the actions taken, as well as the outcomes to be achieved (Stiglitz, 1975, 1977) because "information is imperfect, obtaining information can be costly, [and] there are important asymmetries of information" (Stiglitz, 2000: 1441). Information asymmetry manifests when the knowledge of one actor in a transaction seems inferior to that of the other party regarding the counterparty's true intentions and planned activities (Mas-Colell, Whinston, & Green, 1995; Spence, 1976 A, B, C) or the quality of exchanged goods (Akerlof, 1970). Examples of the latter include employers who may be eager to know a potential employee's abilities prior to the job offer (Stiglitz, 2000), boards of directors that lack sufficient knowledge on the characteristics of external CEO candidates (Zajac, 1990), as well as investors who want to know the true value of a firm before they purchase or merge with it (Capron & Shen, 2007) or invest in it (Cohen & Dean, 2005). Research has identified ways that may be used to overcome information asymmetry. They include establishment of contingency or bounded contracting and monitoring (e.g., see Kreps, 1997; Wiseman & Gómez-Mejía, 1998); signaling, which refers to the active conveyance of information by the knowledgeable party; and/or screening (the active request for additional information by the uninformed party and cooperation (Moro, Fink, & Maresch, 2015).

Even though the micro and psychological perspectives of followership have not examined asymmetric information involving leaders and followers and how that influences their behaviors, the vertical relational structures of the leader–follower exchange suggest that leaders and followers may be privy to different information. The differences may manifest with regard to accuracy, costs, and significance of the information. Followers who have inaccurate information are likely to behave in ways that generate suboptimal outcomes. Costly information may also constrain the effort of followers. Information that is judged to be insignificant may not be utilized even if it may generate valuable outcomes.

Research shows that in the context of group decision-making such as in the leader–follower dyad, asymmetries in information prior to group decision-making and asymmetries in the processing of information during group decision-making interact in relating to group decision quality and associated outcomes (Brodbeck, Kerschreiter, Mojzisch, & Schulz-Hardt, 2007).

Information asymmetry limits knowledge of both followers and leaders. The limitation includes acquisition as well as development. A follower who has incomplete information because of asymmetry is unlikely to transform the information into knowledge that can be effectively used to generate outcomes for constituents in the relational interface. It also affects the ability of a follower to enact his or her role effectively. Police, as informants, depend on communities (as principals) to provide information that will enable them to perform their tasks effectively. To the extent that the communities do not provide information about a particular crime, the police, as followers, may not be able to execute their tasks effectively. In short, information in the form of instructions for task execution, new discoveries that facilitate creativity, or research findings that enhance practice is instrumental to follower role execution. Research examining information asymmetric is likely to enhance understanding of specific relational outcomes that are shaped by or magnified by symmetric information or diminished by asymmetric information. For example, the distribution of information between the leader and the follower is likely to result in differential performance.

4.1.5 Prospect Theory

Another theoretical lens that can be used to examine strategic followership is prospect theory. In 1979, Kahneman and Tversky presented a critique of expected utility theory as a descriptive model of decision-making under risk and developed an alternative model, which they called prospect theory. Kahneman and Tversky summarize several centuries' worth of findings and insights concerning human decision behavior (Kahneman & Tversky, 1979). They found empirically that people underweight outcomes that are merely probable in comparison with outcomes that are obtained with certainty and that people generally discard components that are shared by all prospects under consideration. Prospect theory is a descriptive behavioral theory. It shows that people decide between alternatives that involve risk and uncertainty (e.g. percentage of likelihood of gains or losses). In that regard, it demonstrates what a person thinks in terms of expected utility relative to a reference point (e.g. current achievement) rather than absolute outcomes. The theory was developed as part of framing risky choices. It posits that people are loss-averse, and

74 *Strategic Decisions and Actions*

since individuals dislike losses more than equivalent gains, they are more willing to take risks in order to avoid a loss.

Since then, studies have "produced an unmatched yield of new insights and predictions of human behavior in decision making" (Hastie & Dawes, 2001: 310). At the center of the theory is biased weighting of probabilities and loss aversion (Kahneman, 2011). The theory assigns value to gains and losses rather than to final assets, and probabilities are substituted by decision weights. The value function, defined by deviations from a reference point, is normally concave for gains (implying risk aversion) but convex for losses (risk seeking). Furthermore, it is steeper for losses than for gains (loss aversion). Last, decision weights tend to be lower than the corresponding probabilities, except in the range of low probabilities.

Strategic followership theory is similar to prospect theory in a number of ways even though they have different foci. First, both have a value function. However, unlike prospect theory, where value is assigned to gains and losses, value is assigned to tangible and intangible assets in strategic followership. The inclusion of tangible elements suggests that strategic followership is broader. Second, prospect theory uses decision weights while strategic followership uses probabilities. A strategic follower computes the probabilities associated with restorative and transcendent behaviors likely to be associated with the value of a specific asset. More valued assets have higher weighted probabilities. Third, both use a reference point. In strategic followership theory, the reference point is normal or operative demands prescribed by the follower and leader roles. In other words, there are expected behaviors associated with the follower and leader roles to which each must conform. In the organizational context, leaders are not supposed to influence their subordinates badly. To the extent that a leader does so, a follower is expected to take actions that restore the value that is diminished as a result of such behavior. More concretely, if a leader behaves in a way that damages the reputation of the organization, a restorative follower engages in reputation-building behaviors.

In prospect theory, the reference point is zero or the status quo; it is not bounded, in contrast to strategic followership theory, where the reference point is bounded within the conventional standard deviations. Strategic followership theory recognizes that the conditions of the specific exchange define the zone of normalcy (Zoogah, 2014) such that in one exchange, the zone might be narrow and in another exchange it might be wide. Such a zone does not exist in prospect theory. Fourth, both have convex and concave functions. However, while the function is based on gains and losses, in strategic followership the function is based on restorative and transcendent behaviors. Restorative behaviors are convex because of the value diminishment while transcendent behaviors are concave because of the value enhancement. Gains and losses that may result from restorative and transcendent behaviors were not originally included in strategic followership, which suggests that future research may determine such outcomes. Indeed, gains such as increases in restorative value may be empirically determined as the difference between prior restorative behavior (RB_p) and extant restorative behavior (RB_e; i.e., $\Delta RB_e - RB_p$). Last, strategic followership is relatively narrow compared to prospect theory; the latter is multidisciplinary while the follower centers on followership. Gains and losses manifest in economics, psychology, marking, sociology, anthropology, politics, and so on. As a result, the concavity and relative flatness of the gains function (implying risk aversion) and convexity and steepness of the loss function (risk seeking or loss aversion) can be examined from a broader context.

These differences suggest that empirical research can extend strategic followership theory. Studies on the risks associated with restorative and transcendent followership can be investigated using prospect theory reasoning. The decision weights of prospect theory can be integrated with the probabilities of strategic followership theory. Studies comparing the zone of normalcy of strategic followership can be compared with the single reference point of prospect theory to determine the validity of the zone. Behaviors similar to those observed in economics such as the disposition effect (i.e., the tendency of investors to realize gains but are reluctant to realize losses) or the reversing of risk aversion/risk seeking in case of gains or losses (termed the reflection effect), which can be explained using prospect theory (Kahneman, 2013), may also be examined in strategic followership. For example, is it a natural disposition of some followers to be restorative when they should be transcendent or vice versa? Are some followers more restorative than transcendent? Besides the principal and triggering condition—bad leadership—are there other conditions within which restorative and transcendent followership manifest? These questions are important in advancing strategic followership.

4.2 Strategic Actions

Strategic actions are behaviors that result in strategic outcomes. I break the outcomes into transactional, transformational, and game-theoretic actions. Transactional actions are short-term oriented; they focus on specific outcomes or goals. Restorative actions such as discernment and voice are transactional for two reasons. First, they are time-dependent. Discernment of a situation is more effective when it occurs immediately. Voice for or against a situation (e.g., leader bad behavior) is more potent when it is expressed in tempo. Second, they are outcome-specific in the sense that they focus on knowledge acquisition (discernment) and appropriateness (voice). Transformational actions are long-term oriented; they do not seek to achieve more than short-term outcomes; they focus on total transformation. One example is reparation of harm.

76 *Strategic Decisions and Actions*

Unlike mechanical or physical objects, relationships take a longer time to repair. More effective repairs take a longer time because of the change of state brought about by the harm committed by the leader. These non-zero-sum games differ from game theoretic ones that involve win–lose situations. Zoogah (2014) suggests that the latter are based on the subterfuge path. For organizations, strategic actions may be market-, regulation-, and operations-centered. Market-centered strategic actions are actions that following organizations take to yield specific market outcomes. Regulation-centered strategic actions are those induced by specific regulations. For example, an organization in a following role that complies with anti-trust rules is behaving strategically because of legal requirements. Operations-centered strategic actions are intended to facilitate execution of the organization's operations. They may also include behaviors that are calculative as in zero-sum games. Consequently, I focus on the theoretical perspectives that center on the strategic role action (behavior). Such theories can be used to examine the behavior of strategic followers. I draw from the large number of macro theories that have been used to understand the actions of organizational executives (strategic leadership). Some of these theories include network theory, routine theory, culture theory, institutional theory, and resource-based view. Other theories include stakeholder and agency.

4.2.1 Strategic Behavior Theory

Two theories that can be applied to the strategic decisions of followers are Oliver's (1991) strategic response behavior theory and Child's (1972, 1997) strategic choice theory. First, strategic response theory applies the convergent insights of institutional and resource dependence perspectives to the prediction of strategic responses of organizations to institutional processes. Oliver (1991) offers a typology of strategic responses that vary in active resistance from passive conformity to proactive manipulation. The strategic responses include acquiescence, compromise, avoidance, defiance, and manipulation. Determining these responses are five major factors (cause, constituents, content, control, and context) with two minor factors. These factors are hypothesized to predict the occurrence of the alternative proposed strategies and the degree of organizational conformity or resistance to institutional pressures. Legitimacy and efficiency are principal causes of strategic responses in much the same way that the multiplicity and dependence of constituents determine how organizations respond to institutional pressures. Consistency and constraint are content factors that indicate how an organization responds to pressures. Control factors include coercion and diffusion while uncertainty and interconnectedness represent context. It is the degree (low vs. high) of these factors that determines the type of strategic response. Acquiescence is likely to be adopted when the legitimacy and efficiency are high. However, low multiplicity of constituents and high degree of dependence will also result in an acquiescence response. Strategic response theory is principally at the organizational level. However, the decisions of strategic followers can be studied from strategic response theories. First, the particular strategies that are adopted by followers in response to bad and good leadership behaviors can be examined. Zoogah (2012b) for example, examine the strategic responses of followers to bad leadership. He presented scenarios of bad leadership to participants who, after reading, were asked to choose one strategy in response to the bad leadership situation. Using probit analysis, he regressed the strategic responses to personal and relational determinants and found that moral rectitude was one driver of the strategic response of followers.

The strategic options for followers, for example, can be examined with regard to their effectiveness. First, followers may avoid leaders in the hope that time will 'heal the wounds.' Of course, avoidance is based on trust, not of the leader but of time. However, time may not 'work on the leader.' More important, avoidance is not a constructive relationship building strategy because it ignores the problem between the follower and the leader. Furthermore, the daily contact between followers and leaders suggests that avoidance is not practical because of the possibility of the follower encountering the leader. A better choice is a strategy that is constructive: manipulative. A manipulative strategy seems to be the most active response to pressures buffering followers because it is intended to actively change or exert power over the expectations or the sources that seek to enforce them. Manipulation in this context refers to the purposeful and opportunistic attempt to co-opt, influence, or control leader demands and evaluations. In response to leader demands, a follower may choose to co-opt the source of the pressure (Oliver, 1991). A follower may, for example, attempt to persuade a leader's constituents to join him or her in opposing the leader. The intended effect of co-optation tactics is to neutralize a leader's opposition and to enhance legitimacy. Influence tactics may be more generally directed toward the values and beliefs or definitions and criteria of a leader's demands. A follower may also strategically influence the standards by which he or she is evaluated. This is because the criteria and definitions of performance are often open to strategic reinterpretation and manipulation. Controlling tactics, by comparison, are specific efforts to establish power and dominance over the leader and/or constituents that are applying pressure on the follower. Control is a more actively aggressive response to a leader's pressure than co-optation and influence because the follower's objective is to dominate rather than to influence, shape, or neutralize bad leader demand sources or processes. A follower is more likely to use controlling tactics when a leader's expectations are incipient or weakly promoted. In sum, manipulation involves the active intent to use a leader's demands

78 Strategic Decisions and Actions

and pressures opportunistically, to co-opt and neutralize constituents, to shape and redefine leader–follower norms and external criteria of evaluation, and to control or dominate the source, allocation, or expression of social approval and legitimation.

4.2.2 Resource-Based View

First, organizations gain competitive advantage by leveraging resources. The resource-based theories—organizational capabilities or competence (Pierce, Boerner, & Teece, 2008), resource-based view (Barney, 1991), industry-based (Porter, 1980); neoclassical microeconomics (Ricardo, 1817), and evolutionary economics (Nelson & Winter, 1982)—all show the invaluable characteristic of resources that proffers strategic advantages to individuals, groups, and organizations. Without that characteristic a resource would not be valuable. Thus, a financier who provides finances to an organization occupies a strategic role to that organization; the financier is valued for his or her ability to enable the organization to be defined in a certain way, behave in a particular manner, achieve some outcomes, and function within a specific setting. Assets that do not facilitate these attributes cannot perform this role. In that regard, the entity that possesses resources instantiates a relational exchange where the strategic follower is the actor seeking the resources, and the resource establishes the strategic role.

The capabilities or competence theories (Pierce et al., 2008) have relevance for strategic followership because they center on the ability of followers to function effectively in the relationship, engage in either restorative or transcendent behaviors, make decisions that would likely lead to valuable outcomes, and manipulate the relational environment to generate the desired goals. Furthermore, given the changes in the relational environment, dynamic capabilities, defined as a set of specific and identifiable processes such as strategic decision-making and collaborating, can be used to understand not only the decisions of a strategic follower (e.g., organization) but also the behavior of that actor. Within the strategy literature, dynamic capabilities drive the creation, evolution, and recombination of other resources into new sources of competitive advantage (Henderson & Cockburn, 1994; Teece et al., 1997). At the firm level, Eisenhardt and Martin (2000) define dynamic capabilities as a "firm's processes that use resources—specifically the processes to integrate, reconfigure, gain and release resources—to match and even create market change" (p. 1107). The transactive relations between managers of a following and a leading firm are likely to determine the integrations, reconfigurations, and matchings that eventually lead to strategic outcomes (e.g., market changes) that benefit the organization. Applied to strategic followership, dynamic capabilities refer to the transactive processes by which a follower deploys tangible (e.g., psychological) and intangible resources (e.g., time) to integrate or restructure relational resources to match the leader -follower relationship to yield superior outcomes for relational constituents. Defined from this perspective, dynamic capabilities apply to organizational and individual entities in followership role.

4.2.3 Network Theory

Network theory has become so profuse in organization and management literature that it is applied to almost all aspects of organizational life—interactions, production, teams, operations, intra- and interorganizational relations, suppliers, voice, and so on (Borgatti & Halgin, 2011; Westaby, Woods, & Pfaff, 2016). Generally, network theory refers to a connected subset of nodes that is linked to the remaining network (Gulbahce & Lehmann, 2008). A complex network has a densely connected subset of nodes that is only sparsely linked to the remaining network (Fortunato, 2010), and a social network refers to "the mechanisms and processes that interact with network structures to yield certain outcomes for individuals and groups" (Borgatti & Halgin, 2011: 1168). We focus on social network and the specific roles followers may play. Networks are composed of core and peripheral nodes. While the core nodes are central, the peripheral nodes link to other networks or span boundaries. They function in different roles. Followers in network cores have access to information and other resources that can determine how relational outcomes and other value-creating activities can and should be performed. They are able to contribute greater value than those in the peripheral role. However, followers who function as boundary spanners can also facilitate the integration of significant individuals who can contribute value to the relationship or its constituents.

In their study of shared leadership networks, Sullivan, Lungeanu, Dechurch, and Contractor (2015) used shared leadership theory to show how distributed the followership is within a multiteam system. Based on DeRue and Ashford's (2010) leadership co-construction of roles, they suggest that the leader "claims leadership" and that the follower "accepts leadership," a process that is "particularly well-suited to testing with a network perspective—essentially explaining the underlying psychological process through which a directed tie is formed" (p. 4). They "operationalize followership concentration as the out-degree decentralization of leadership reliance ties" (p. 5).

These studies suggest that network theory can be applied to strategic followership. One way to do that is to consider the sets of followers in the organization (i.e., those in the core and periphery) and their contributions (i.e., values). Followers who are closer to bad leaders may engage in more restorative behaviors because of the concern for the leaders and thereby yield greater value than those followers who are relatively more

80 Strategic Decisions and Actions

distant. It seems to be the opposite of the least preferred co-worker theory (Fiedler, 1974) which suggests that followers' value is likely to be greater the denser the networks (i.e., the closer they are to their leaders).

Networks are popular because of the interlinkages between actors. The interlinkages provide advantages and induce strategic behaviors on the part of the actors. Actors in a network have roles, some core and peripheral roles. Those in the core roles have access to information because of the central position they occupy (Borgatti & Halgin, 2011). In other words, they are connectors, binders, or integrators. An exemplar of a connector is a boundary-spanner, a manager who spans two or more organizational boundaries (Andersson & Forsgren, 2000). In strategic alliances, managers who liaise between focal and partner firms connect the organizations in a way that facilitates execution of joint programs. The connecter role is complex in alliances with multiple, rather than dyadic, organizational relationships.

Strategic followership in multiple strategic alliances or networks manifests in two ways. First, if it is an equity alliance a manager representing his or her organization functions as a follower if that organization is following the practices of one or more organizations in the network. The behavior of the manager in that context is based on equality. In the New United Motor Manufacturing, Inc. (NUMMI) equity joint venture between General Motors and Toyota, alliance managers of General Motors, a following firm that wanted to learn the unique practices of Toyota, engaged in strategic actions that facilitated achievement of General Motors' strategic objectives. They embedded and organized activities that enabled General Motors to excel as a small car manufacturer (Inkpen, 1998). Second, if the alliance is a nonequity network, then the organization with minority shares assumes the followership role. The alliance manager in that context behaves strategically either using stratagem (i.e., use of subterfuge in situations that demand actions for which the firm may be unwilling or unable to fulfill) or taking actions that directly effectuate the strategic objectives of the organization.

Two strategic actions that are likely in both equity and nonequity networks are lock-out and lock-in behaviors. Lock-out and lock-in behaviors occur "because in many situations, ties formed with one actor place constraints on ties with others" (Gulati, Nohria, & Zaheer, 2000: 210). The constraints may be due to limited resources or "the expectation the alliance partner may have for fidelity to the alliance, including the exclusion of other partners" (Gulati et al., 2000: 211). Lock-out actions refer to behaviors that result from the choices of a firm to ally with some partners that, ipso facto, exclude others. The partnering decision is strategic and arises from the limited time and resources. Lock-in actions refer to behaviors associated with expectations the alliance partner may have for fidelity to the alliance, including the exclusion of other partners. The focal firm is locked into the exclusive relationship with the partner firm because of the expectation of explicit monogamy that precludes the parties from allying with similar others or an implicit expectation of loyalty. Duysters and Lemmens (2003) also observe that embeddedness in a network that has an enabling effect can be turned into a paralyzing effect as actors become locked in, particularly if they rely on partners only in their closed social system. "Searching for, or switching to, partners outside of the alliance group is not likely, particularly when trustworthy partners are already available in this system" (Duysters & Lemmens, 2003: 49). It is therefore likely that lock-in and lock-out strategic actions can influence strategic followership effectiveness as suggested by the alliance literature which indicates that "these constrained choices in turn can have significant performance consequences".

The second aspect of networks is social capital, the resources inherent in social relations which facilitate collective action or social relations that have productive benefits. Social capital is part of networks definitionally because some consider it "the collective value of all social networks (who people know), and the inclinations that arise from these networks to do things for each other (norms of reciprocity)" (Sanders, 2015). Duyster and Lemmens (2003) "examine the role of embeddedness and social capital in the process of alliance group formation in strategic technology alliance networks" and found that "through the formation of subsequent ties, firms in social systems tend to rely heavily on their direct and indirect contacts in forming new partnerships" (p. 49). Embeddedness is the social mechanisms that enable and enforce the alliance group formation. Their study suggests that the more embedded an organization is in the alliance network, the greater the likelihood that the manager will enact strategic behaviors. Some of these could be lock-in or lock-out actions.

4.2.4 Negotiation Theory

Negotiation theory proposes that the parties in a negotiation sometimes exhibit strategic behavior, particularly when the power dynamics are not balanced. Negotiation theory traditionally centers on negotiation between two or more parties. Because the parties have divergent goals initially, the strategies and moves they adopt enable them to reach convergent points. The effectiveness of each party depends on the strategic moves applied to the specific strategic situations. Three situations applicable to followership include bargaining, brinkmanship, and incentives. In bargaining situations, the leader and the follower try to reach an agreement about a conflicting issue (e.g., exploiting a deal). They prefer that option to inaction and believe that there will be compromise in the process in order to create value. To be effective the leader and the follower have to recognize the knowledge and beliefs of each other, their interdependencies, goals and flexibilities, decision-making abilities, the context of the bargaining process, and the values and behavioral norms undergirding each part. The

82 *Strategic Decisions and Actions*

cognitions (e.g., knowledge structures), emotions, competencies, experiences, and attitudes of leaders and followers affect the bargaining process and outcomes. More important, the leader and the follower have to consider the major factor: the best alternative to a negotiated agreement or best alternative to no agreement (BATNA). It is the best that a follower can get if he or she is not able to reach an agreement with a leader in bargaining. Because best alternatives to negotiated agreements function as minimal, they represent opportunities for the leaders and followers. Strategic followers who observe that better outside opportunities can translate into an increased proportion of the value are likely to adopt strategic moves that improve their outside opportunities. The significance of the outside opportunity is likely to increase if the follower looks at it relative to that of the leader. For example, if the leader's opportunity or best alternative to a negotiated agreement is lower, the follower's commitment and threats are likely to be different. That will result in a different behavior.

Brinkmanship is a negotiating technique in which either party aggressively pursues a set of terms ostensibly to the point at which the other party in the negotiation must either agree or halt negotiations. Brinkmanship is so named because one party pushes the other to the "brink" or edge of what that party is willing to accommodate. It seems more likely that the leader will use such a technique because he is endowed with authority or power. However, it can also be used by the follower particularly if he is influenced either with regard to expertise, memory, or some other unique capability. In this context it is a strategic situation in which the follower pursues positive terms to the point that the leader consents for him or her to enact. By emphasizing the positive, the follower is likely to bring the leader to the brink of acceptance. Brinkmanship tends to be used at the end of a long negotiation, focuses on one issue or a small subset of all issues that composed the negotiation, centers on an impending deadline, and commonly involves a terrible alternative for both parties, yet somehow either the leader or follower convinces the other that he or she is willing to accept that alternative if the other party doesn't agree to its terms.

Incentives are mechanisms that induce a party in a negotiation to act in a particular way. For example, a leader who acts in a bad way and anticipates that the moral rectitude of a follower might lead to him or her being 'reported' may incentivize the follower in his attempt to negotiate his way out of potential reprimand, demotion, or dismissal. As inducements, incentives attempt to alter the moves of a follower such that instead of adopting Strategy A, he or she adopts Strategy B, which is incentivized. Incentives may be pecuniary or nonpecuniary. While a leader may use pecuniary incentives because of his or her access to and control over resources, a follower may deploy nonpecuniary resources such as expertise, loyalty, and commitment. Nonpecuniary resources have equal potency inducing the leader to behave in a particular way.

Summary

These theoretical lenses that can be used to investigate the strategic decisions of followers. I recognize that strategic decision theory, which has been examined extensively in the strategy literature, might be used as a strategic lens. The major driver in strategic followership—strategic situation—is not explicitly a determinant in the strategic management literature. In the words of Davis (1971) the lenses recommended here are intended to extend strategic followership in an interesting way. By looking at the decisions, we can understand the actions of the followers. Psychological research (e.g., theory of reasoned action or theory of planned behavior) shows that the actions of entities (i.e., individuals and groups) do not emerge in a vacuum; they arise from the decisions of those entities.

Note

1. This is a variation of the stag–hare hunt game (see Guastello, 2008).

References

Afzal, W. (2015). Towards the general theory of information asymmetry. In Al-Suqri, M. M. & AlAufi, A. S. (Eds.), *Information Seeking Behavior and Technology Adoption: Theories and Trends* (pp. 124–135). Hershey, PA: IGI Global.

Andersson, U., & Forsgren, M. (2000). In search of centre of excellence: Network embeddedness and subsidiary roles in multinational corporations. *MIR: Management International Review*, 329–350.

Akerlof, G. (1970). The market for lemons: Qualitative uncertainty and the market mechanism. *Quarterly Journal of Economics*, 84(3).

Barney, J. B. (1991). Firm resources and sustained competitive advantage. *Journal of Management*, 17(1), 99–120.

Bliege-Bird, R., & Smith, E. (2005). Signaling theory, strategic interaction, and symbolic capital. *Current Anthropology*, 46(2), 221–248.

Borgatti, S. P., & Halgin, D. S. (2011). On network theory. *Organization Science*, 22(5), 1168–1181.

Brodbeck, F. C., Kerschreiter, R., Mojzisch, A., & Schulz-Hardt, S. (2007). Group decision making under conditions of distributed knowledge: The information asymmetries model. *Academy of Management Review*, 32(2), 459–479.

Capron, L., & Shen, J. C. (2007). Acquisitions of private vs. public firms: Private information, target selection, and acquirer returns. *Strategic Management Journal*, 28(9), 891–911.

Carpentier, C., L'her, J. F., & Suret, J. M. (2010). Stock exchange markets for new ventures. *Journal of Business Venturing*, 25(4), 403–422.

Child, J. (1972). Organizational structure, environments and performance: The role of strategic choice. *Sociology*, 6, 1–22.

Child, J. (1997). Strategic choice in the analysis of action, structure, organizations and environment: Retrospect and prospect. *Organization Studies*, 18(1), 43–76.

84 Strategic Decisions and Actions

Cohen, B. D., & Dean, T. J. (2005). Information asymmetry and investor valuation of IPOs: Top management team legitimacy as a capital market signal. *Strategic Management Journal*, 26(7), 683–690.

Davis, M. S. (1971). That's interesting! Towards a phenomenology of sociology and a sociology of phenomenology. *Philosophy of the Social Sciences*, 1(2), 309–344.

Dawkins, R. (1976). *The Selfish Gene*. Oxford, NY: Oxford University Press.

DeRue, D. S., & Ashford, S. J. (2010). Power to the people: Where has personal agency gone in leadership development? *Industrial and Organizational Psychology*, 3(1), 24–27.

Duysters, G., & Lemmens, C. (2003). Alliance group formation enabling and constraining effects of embeddedness and social capital in strategic technology alliance networks. *International Studies of Management & Organization*, 33(2), 49–68.

Eden, C., Spender, J. C., & Spender, J. C. (Eds.), (1998). *Managerial and Organizational Cognition: Theory, Methods and Research*. California: Sage.

Eisenhardt, K. M., & Martin, J. A. (2000). Dynamic capabilities: What are they? *Strategic Management Journal*, 21(10–11), 1105–1121.

Fiedler, F. E. (1974). The contingency model: New directions for leadership utilization. *Journal of Contemporary Business*, 3(4), 65–79.

Fortunato, S. (2010). Community detection in graphs. *Physics Reports*, 486, 75–174.

Freeman, R. E. (1984). *Strategic Management: A Stakeholder Approach*. Boston: Pitman.

Friedman, D. (1994). Experiments in decision, organization and exchange: Richard H. Day and Vernon L. Smith, eds., (North Holland, Amsterdam, 1993) viii + 380 pp. *Journal of Economic Behavior & Organization*, 24(2), 239–241.

Friedman, D., & Sunder, S. (1994). *Experimental Methods: A Primer for Economists*. Cambridge University Press.

Guastello, S. J. (2008). Chaos and Conflict: Recognizing Patterns. *Emergence: Complexity & Organization*, 10(4).

Guastello, S. J., Bock, B. R., Caldwell, P., & Bond Jr, R. W. (2005). Origins of group coordination: Nonlinear dynamics and the role of verbalization. *Nonlinear Dynamics, Psychology, and Life Sciences*.

Guastello, S. J., & Bond Jr, R. W. (2007). The emergence of leadership in coordination-intensive groups. *Nonlinear Dynamics, Psychology, and Life Sciences*.

Guastello, S. J., & Guastello, D. D. (1998). Origins of coordination and team effectiveness: A perspective from game theory and nonlinear dynamics. *Journal of Applied Psychology*, 83(3), 423.

Gulati, R., Nohria, N., & Zaheer, A. (2000). Strategic networks. *Strategic Management Journal*, 21(3), 203–215.

Gulbahce, N., & Lehmann, S. (2008). The art of community detection. *BioEssays*, 30(10), 934–938.

Hadley, C. N., Pittinsky, T. L., Sommer, S. A., & Zhu, W. (2009). Measuring the efficacy of leaders to assess information and make decisions in a crisis: The CLEAD scale. Center for Public Leadership. Unpublished Technical report (RWP09-021).

Hastie, R., & Dawes, R. M. (2001). *Rational Decision in an Uncertainty World: The Psychology of Judgment and Decision Making*. Thousand Oaks, CA: Sage.

Henderson, R., & Cockburn, I. (1994). Measuring competence? Exploring firm effects in pharmaceutical research. Strategic Management Journal, 15(S1), 63–84.

Hodgkinson, G. P., & Healey, M. P. (2008). Cognition in Organizations. *Annual Review of Psychology*, 59, 387–417.

Inkpen, A. C. (1998). Learning and knowledge acquisition through international strategic alliances. *Academy of Management Perspectives*, 12(4), 69–80.

Kahneman, D. (2013). *Think, Fast and Slow*. New York: Farrar, Straus and Giroux.

Kahneman, D. (2011). *Thinking, Fast and Slow*. New York, NY: MacMillan

Kahneman, D., & Tversky, A. (1979). On the interpretation of intuitive probability: A reply to Jonathan Cohen. *Cognition*, 7(4), 409–411. http://dx.doi. org/10.1016/0010-0277(79)90024-

Kahneman, D., & Tversky, A. (1973). On the psychology of prediction. *Psychological review*, 80(4), 237.

Keating, M. E., Pruitt, D. G., Eberle, R. A., & Mikolic, J. M. (1994). Strategic choice in everyday disputes. *International Journal of Conflict Management*, 5(2), 143–157.

Kreps, D. M. (1997). Intrinsic motivation and extrinsic incentives. *The American Economic Review*, 87(2), 359–364.

Lazarus, R. S., Folkman, S. (1984). Coping and adaptation. In Gentry, W. D. (Ed.), *The Handbook of Behavioural Medicine* (pp. 282–325). New York: Guilford.

Leslie, L. M., & Gelfand, M. J. (2012). The cultural psychology of social influence: Implications for organizational politics. In Ferris, G. R. & Treadway, D. C. (Eds.), *Politics in Organizations: Theory and Research Considerations* (pp. 411–447). New York: Taylor Francis Publishing.

Leslie, L. M., & Gelfand, M. J. (2011). The cultural psychology of social influence: Implications for organizational politics. In Ferris, G. R. & Treadway, D. C. (Eds.), *Politics in Organizations: Theory and Research Considerations* (pp. 411–447). New York: Taylor Francis Publishing.

Leventhal, H., Meyer, D., & Nerenz, D. (1980). The common sense model of illness representation danger. In Rachman, S. (Ed.), *Medical Psychology*, (Vol. 2, pp. 7–30). New York: Pergamon Press.

Luthans, F., Luthans, K. W., & Luthans, B. C. (2004). Positive psychological capital: Human and social capital. *Business Horizons*, 47(1), 45–50.

Mas-Colell, A., Whinston, M. D., & Green, J. R. (1995). *Microeconomic Theory*. Oxford, UK: Oxford University Press.

Maynard-Smith, J. (1982). *Evolution and the Theory of Games*. Cambridge, England: Cambridge University Press.

Mintzberg, H., Ahlstrand, B. W., & Lampel, J. (1998). *Strategy Safari: The Complete Guide Through the Wilds of Strategic Management*. Harlow, UK: Financial Times, Prentice Hall.

Moro, A., Fink, M., & Maresch, D. (2015). Reduction in information asymmetry and credit access for small and medium-sized enterprises. *Journal of Financial Research*, 38(1), 121–143.

Nelson, R. R., & Winter, S. G. (1982). The Schumpeterian tradeoff revisited. *The American Economic Review*, 72(1), 114–132.

Oliver, C. (1991). Strategic responses to institutional processes. *Academy of Management Review*, 16(1), 145–179.

86 Strategic Decisions and Actions

Pearson, C. M., & Clair, J. A. (1998). Reframing crisis management. *Academy of Management Review*, 23(1), 59–76.

Pierce, J. L., Boerner, C. S., Teece, D. J., Augier, M., & March, J. G. (2008). Dynamic capabilities, competence and the behavioral theory of the firm. *Technological Know-How, Organizational Capabilities, and Strategic Management*, 53–68.

Porter, M. (1980). *Corporate Strategy*. New York, NY. Free Press.

Ricardo, D. (1817). *Principles of Political Economy and Taxation*. London: J. Murray.

Sanders, J. (2015). *Adaptation and Appropriation*. New York: Routledge.

Schippers, M., Rook, L., & van de Velde, S. (2011). Crisis performance predictability in supply chains. *RSM Discovery-Management Knowledge*, 7(3), 10–11.

Snyder, C., Irving, L. M., & Anderson, S. A. (1991). Hope and health: Measuring the will and the ways. In Snyder, C. R. & Forsyth, D. R. (Eds.), *Handbook of Social and Clinical Psychology: The Health Perspective* (pp. 285–305). Elmsford, NY: Pergamon.

Spence, M. (1976). Informational aspects of market structure: An introduction. *The Quarterly Journal of Economics*, 591–597.

Stiglitz, J. E. (1975). The theory of "screening," education, and the distribution of income. *The American Economic Review*, 65(3), 283–300.

Stiglitz, J. E. (1977). Monopoly, non-linear pricing and imperfect information: The insurance market. *The Review of Economic Studies*, 44(3), 407–430.

Stiglitz, J. E. (2000). The contributions of the economics of information to twentieth century economics. *The Quarterly Journal of Economics*, 115(4), 1441–1478.

Sullivan, S. D., Lungeanu, A., Dechurch, L. A., & Contractor, N. S. (2015). Space, time, and the development of shared leadership networks in multiteam systems. *Network Science*, 3(1), 124–155.

Sweeney, K. (2008). Crisis decision theory: Decisions in the face of negative events. *Psychological Bulletin*, 134, 61–76.

Teece, D. J., Pisano, G., & Shuen, A. (1997). Dynamic capabilities and strategic management. *Strategic Management Journal*, 18(7), 509–533.

Turner, J. E., Goodin, J. B., & Lokey, C. (2012). Exploring the roles of emotions, motivations, self-efficacy, and secondary control following critical unexpected life events. *Journal of Adult Development*, 19(4), 215–227.

Walsh, J. P. (1995). Managerial and organizational cognition: Notes from a trip down memory lane. *Organization Science*, 6(3), 280–321.

Van Vugt, M. (2006). Evolutionary origins of leadership and followership. *Personality and Social Psychology Review*, 10(4), 354–371.

Van Vugt, M., Hogan, R., & Kaiser, R. B. (2008). Leadership, followership and evolution: Some lessons from the past. *American Psychologist*, 63(3), 182.

Westaby, J. D., Woods, N., & Pfaff, D. L. (2016). Extending dynamic network theory to group and social interaction analysis: Uncovering key behavioral elements, cycles, and emergent states. *Organizational Psychology Review*, 6(1), 34–62.

Wiseman, R. M., & Gomez-Mejia, L. R. (1998). A behavioral agency model of managerial risk taking. *Academy of Management Review*, 23(1), 133–153.

Zagare, F. C. (1984). *Game Theory: Concepts and Applications*. Beverley Hills, CA: Sage.

Zajac, E. J. (1990). CEO selection, succession, compensation and firm performance: A theoretical integration and empirical analysis. *Strategic Management Journal*, 11(3), 217–230.

Zoogah, D. B. (Ed.), (2014). *Advancing Research Methodology in the African Context: Techniques, Methods, and Designs*. Bingley, UK: Emerald Group Publishing.

Zoogah, D. B. (2012a). Strategic management research in emerging economies: A lens model perspective. In *West Meets East: Toward Methodological Exchange* (pp. 35–72). Emerald Group Publishing Limited.

Zoogah, D. B. (2012b, August). Strategic followership and follower effectiveness. Paper Presented at the Academy of Management Annual Meeting, Boston, Massachusetts.

5   Strategic Interactions

How do the relational transactions of followers manifest to yield outcomes for constituents in the relational interface? The interactions involving followers and leaders are strategic to the extent that they involve restorative and transcendent transactions that generate value for constituents in the relational interface. They are shaped by strategic cognition and strategic affect. Theories that relate to strategic interactions, strategic cognition, and strategic affect are discussed. They can be used to understand the two paths—mediated and direct—of strategic followership.

5.1 Strategic Interactions

Strategic interactions center on the cognitions and behaviors of followers and leaders as firms (firm level) and subordinates (individual level). The ability of a follower to achieve strategic outcomes depends on how it deploys cognitive and behavioral mechanisms to affect the behavior of the leader. Leadership and followership generally focus on the process by which either a leader or a follower induces the other to change his or her behavior toward accomplishing some specified objectives (Lubit, 2004; Ross, 1991). Yukl (1989: 5) defines leadership as "influence processes involving determination of the group's or organization's objectives, motivating task behavior in pursuit of these objectives, and influencing group maintenance and culture." Barling (2014) also views followership as an influence process in which the follower attempts to alter the behavior of a leader toward a specific objective. Rost (2008: 57) defines collaborative leadership as "an influence relationship among leaders and collaborators who intend significant changes that reflect their mutual interests" because he views "followers" as "collaborators."

Influence, the capacity of a follower to persuade a leader to submit to what the follower wants and intends, of the leader's own volition (Kellerman, 2012) has diverse dimensions (social, cultural, economic, political, and psychological—Cialdini, 1993) and levels. Inter-actor influence applies to individual and firms. For the former, the interpersonal relationship literature (see Kenny and La Voie, 1984) shows that individuals

Strategic Interactions 89

influence each other during interactions. For the latter, representatives of firms—CEO, board of directors, top management—often function as informants as suggested by the strategy and strategic leadership literature (Finkelstein et al., 2009). The literature on interfirm interactions has principally focused on partnerships, strategic alliances, and buyer–supplier relationship where coordination, cooperation, and communication are major factors (Hall, Clark, Giordano, Johnson, & van Roekel, 1977; Hardy & Phillips, 1998; Schmidt & Kochan, 1977).

I define strategic interaction as the transfer of energy between leader and follower where energy refers to the forceful inducement by the follower of the leader.[1] I view strategic interactions as a function of resource endowment such that the relationship between a follower and a leader may be characterized by dependency. According to Hirschhorn (1990), authority (dependency) models are 'internalized models' that are enacted across various roles and positions. Consistent with that view, firms, for example, have internalized models of dependency relations that shape how they behave in social systems. Using Kahn and Kram's (1994) typology of enduring internalized models of authority—dependence, counterdependence, and interdependence—I argue that both leading and following firms may relate with each other out of dependency, "deauthorizing themselves to take responsibility for managing themselves" (p. 28). In counterdependency, both leading and following firms 'dismiss or undermine the determined role interactions' and 'seek to step outside the boundaries of role-determined relations' (p. 29). For interdependent interactions, following and leading firms depend on the authority ascriptions of the roles as well as independence from that authority. The combination of the follower's dependency orientation and the leader's dependency orientation results in nine forms of strategic interactions and influence dynamics. As shown in Table 5.1 some interactions are symmetric with regard to the orientations while others are asymmetric. In symmetric interactions, both followers and leaders have equal orientations—interdependence, dependency, and counterdependency. In asymmetric interactions, either one has an inferior or superior orientation toward the interaction. I begin with symmetric interactions.

5.1.1 Symmetric Interactions

The first symmetric interaction is one of interdependence. When both following and leading firms interact out of interdependence, the influence dynamic is one of equality (FF = LF). Sharing of information thus becomes a potent influence tactic likely to be used by a following firm because it facilitates effective interactions. The information asymmetry and negotiation literature show the significance of information exchange not only for influencing other parties but also for achieving strategic

90 Strategic Interactions

Table 5.1 Influence Dynamics, Tactics, and Theoretical Lenses for Inter-organizational Interaction Orientation

		Following Firm (FF)		
		Interdependent	*Dependent*	*Counterdependent*
Leading firm (LF)	*Interdependent*	Dynamic: FF = LF Tactics: Information exchange Cooperation	Dynamic: FF < LF Tactics: Build trust Active participation Reliability	Dynamic: FF > LF Tactic: Information control Nonconformity
	Dependency	Dynamic: FF > LF Tactics: Empathy Modeling Authenticity	Dynamic: FF = LF Tactics: Pleas Requests Coalition	Dynamic: FF > LF Tactics: Recommendation Competence
	Counter-dependent	Dynamic: FF < LF Tactics Monitoring Consultation	Dynamic: FF < LF Tactics: Proactivity Ingratiation Promises	Dynamic: FF = LF Tactics: Threats Demands Warning

Source: Compiled from Howell and Mendez (2008); Tangpong, Michalisin, Traub, and Melcher (2015); Möllering (2003); Laing and Lian (2005); Tong, Van Der Heide, Langwell, and Walther (2008); Macneil (1980a, 1980b); Kaufmann and Stern (1988); Frazier and Summers (1984, 1986); Kale (1986, 1989); and Frazier and Rody (1991).

outcomes. For example, Raes, Heijltjes, Glunk, and Roe (2011) propose a process model of the interface between top management and middle managers where information exchange is central to the influence process. Studies in the resource dependence (Casciaro & Piskorski, 2005), social networks (Jones, Hesterly, & Borgatti, 1997), and symbolism (Bliege-Bird & Smith, 2005) show the importance of information exchange as an influence mechanism. Another influence tactic is cooperation, the act or instance of acting together for a common purpose or benefit. Cooperation induces suppliance of the leader. The degree to which both the leader and the follower are cooperative thus enables the interaction to yield desired outcomes. In that regard, cooperative behaviors induce mutual influence.

The second symmetric interaction is dependence. It is defined by the influence dynamic of equality because both following and leading firms need each other. Consequently, influence tactics such as pleas, requests, conformity, and coalitions are likely to be used. A follower pleads with a leader not only to act consistent with expectations but also to make decisions that facilitate achievement of strategic outcomes. Consistent with Frazier and Summers (1984) a follower may use legalistic pleas to contend that a leader's compliance is required by formal agreement. In addition to pleas, requests that are solicitations from a follower to a leader may be used. As influence tactics, requests tend to be used in contexts of dependency (Cialdini, 1984). Last, coalition, an influence mechanism that involves the combination of a following and leader on a temporary basis, is used to define a common position, interest, or course of action. The convergence of interests has a component of strategic utility: the consensual acceptance of an outcome because it is backed by both parties to defeat other possible outcomes (Coleman, 1990).

The third symmetric interaction is counterdependence. Counterdependent interactions occur when both leaders and followers oppose, dismiss or undermine the determined role interactions and step outside the boundaries of role-determined relations. Because counterdependence is associated with greater power, each party is likely to use influence tactics such as threats, demands, and warnings. Threat, an influence mechanism where a follower informs a leader that failure to comply is likely to result in negative sanctions, is common in the interpersonal and interfirm relationship literature (Galaskiewicz, 1985; Kenny and La Voie, 1984). Frazier and Summers (1986), as well as Kale (1986), showed that threat is a coercive tactic that is often used by firms to alter the behavior of other firms. Another tactic is demand where a follower asks for something from a leader using an authoritative instrument. A demand is a claim as a right and derives from the power associated with the follower or leader. It is a relatively coercive mechanism that is laden with expectations. Studies of tournaments show that competitors increasingly make demands that influence the behavior of the parties (Camerer & Weber, 2013). Last, warning, an intimation of possible harm or anything else unfavorable to a leader, also occurs when the follower is counterdependent. The ability to warn the leader is the basis for the tactic and it arises when the follower perceives that the leader is interacting in a way that jeopardizes potential strategic outcomes.

5.1.2 Asymmetric Interaction I

The first asymmetric interaction is where the follower has an inferior orientation. As shown in Table 5.1, there are three instances when that may occur. When the follower is dependent on the leader and the latter has an interdependent orientation, the influence dynamic (FF < LF) is unequal. The subordinate position of the follower suggests that influence tactics such as trust building, active involvement in the relational

92 Strategic Interactions

exchange, and demonstration of reliability is likely to dissuade the leader to behave in a way that will enable the relationship to achieve its strategic outcomes. Trust building is a major influence mechanism in the negotiation (Koeszegi, 2004), social capital (Adler & Kwon, 2000), and justice (Sabel, 1993) literature. Related to trust is reliability. To the extent that a leader finds a follower as reliable, it is likely to act affirmatively toward the follower. The organizational behavior literature also shows that active participation is a mechanism that affects actors' views and behaviors (Etzioni, 1975).

A second instance is when the follower is dependent but the leader has a counterdependent orientation. The ability of the leader to walk away from the relationship because of the leverage it has suggests the influence dynamic (FF < LF) is unequal. Influence tactics such as proactivity, ingratiation, and promise are likely to affect a leader's behavior. Proactivity, acting on the interacting environment in a self-directed way to bring about change, such as by showing initiative, preventing problems, and scanning for opportunities to advance the relationship (see Strauss, Griffin, & Rafferty, 2009), is important in leadership (Strauss et al., 2009) and interfirm relationships (Kowalkowski, Witell, & Gustafsson, 2013). The political (Leslie & Gelfand, 2012), stakeholder (Garcés-Ayerbe, Rivera-Torres, & Murillo-Luna, 2012), and agency (Liu, Sun, Dix, & Narasipuram, 2001) literatures show proactivity as important in the conversion of constituents, advocacy of interest, and representation of principals respectively. Ingratiation, a tactic that is intended to evoke interfirm liking and attraction between the follower and the leader, involves the use of "behaviors that are designed to enhance one's interpersonal attractiveness" and improve rapport with the target of influence (Kumar & Beyerlein, 1991: 619). These actions consist primarily of compliments toward the leader for his/her achievements (other enhancement) and expressing attitude similarity (Kipnis & Schmidt, 1988; Kipnis, Schmidt, & Wilkinson, 1980). Promise, where the follower pledges to provide the leader with a specific reward contingent on the leader's compliance with the follower's request (Frazier & Summers, 1984: 46), induces in the leader a reward expectation consistent with compliance. Promises are thus pledges of future rewards for the leader.

The third instance is when the follower has an interdependent orientation but the leader has a counterdependent orientation. Given that counterdependence seems superior to interdependence in relationships (Kahn & Kram, 1994), the influence dynamic (FF < LF) is unequal. The follower can employ monitoring and consultation tactics. Monitoring, the process of observing the follower's relational environment to detect issues of concern, is an influence tactic (Higgins & Judge, 2004). It induces in the leader an appreciation to advance the relationship rather than walk away. Consultation, the process of seeking advice or information from the leader or having regard for the leader in decision-making, is an upward influence tactic that is useful in relationships characterized by superior–subordinate relations. Cable and Judge (2003) found that managers trying to influence leaders will be more likely to employ influence tactics that emphasize consultation. A follower that consults a leader is likely to inspire the latter.

5.1.3 Asymmetric Interaction II

The second asymmetric interaction is where the follower has a superior orientation. As shown in Table 5.1, there are three instances when that may occur. First, a follower with an interdependent orientation seems superior to a leader that has a dependent orientation. The dynamic (FF > LF) is unequal but favorable toward the follower. A follower is able to affect the behavior of a leader through influence tactics such as empathy, modeling, and authenticity. Consistent with Parasuraman, Zeithaml, and Berry (1988), empathy, a neglected but key influence tactic, refers to the attention a follower provides to a leader. It shows the sensitivity of the follower to the leader (Pfeffer, 1992). A highly empathetic firm is able to understand, predict, and adapt to the challenges associated with the relationship (Redmond, 1989). Behavioral modeling refers to a follower's demonstration of desired behaviors based on observation and replication of the leader's behavior. Because inspiration often requires modeling behavior and setting an example for others to follow, a behavioral model as an influence tactic manifests through inspirational appeals. A follower who has an interdependent orientation is likely to inspire a leader who has a dependent orientation. In other words, the follower may model its orientation to the dependent leader. Authenticity, here defined as the state of being in which a follower's self is highly integrated and its behaviors are felt to be in line with its beliefs and values (Kernis & Goldman, 2006), is an influence tactic. In other words, the follower has a sense of being able to express and act on its true self during its interactions with the leader. It involves awareness, unbiased processing, behavior, and relational orientation of the follower (Kernis & Goldman, 2006).

Another orientation is where a follower with a counterdependent orientation has interaction with a leader that has a dependent orientation. The dynamic (FF > LF) is unequal but favorable toward the follower. Given that the follower is counterdependent and the leader is dependent, a follower can use recommendation and competence as influence tactics. Recommendations are arguments used to convince a leader that the decisions and actions of either the follower or leader would be beneficial to the leader (Venkatesh, Kohli, & Zaltman, 1995). Boyle and Dwyer (1995), for example, used Frazier and Summers (1984) typology of interfirm relationships to suggest that recommendations have a positive effect on the performance of the interfirm relationship. Recommendations that are potentially valuable to the leader's operations increase the follower's

94 *Strategic Interactions*

reputation as an expert and a means for future success. Unlike recommendations, competence is a tacit appeal that relies on the capabilities of the follower. To the extent that the follower demonstrates unique attributes of skill and expertise that is wanting in the leader, the latter is likely to be induced to alter its behavior. In that regard, competence is an inspirational appeal. Research shows that expert power is an influence mechanism (French, Raven, & Cartwright, 1959).

Furthermore, a follower with a counterdependent orientation may interact with a leader who has an interdependent orientation. The dynamic (FF > LF) is unequal and oriented favorably toward the follower. Two influence tactics are information control and nonconformity. Information control refers to the capacity of a follower to regulate information or a follower's ability to exert control over a leader's use of shared information for purposes not anticipated by the relationship. It differs to some extent from information exchange, which focuses on sharing information with no specific action requested or otherwise indicated (Leifer & Mills, 1996). It is a coercive, rather than noncoercive, tactic. Conformity, defined as a change in opinions or behaviors of a leader to match those of follower, generally includes acquiescence and acceptance. It is a positive influence. However, nonconformity defined as a follower's refusal to change its opinion or behavior can affect a leader. As a form of resistance nonconformity manifests through dissent—acting according to the firm's beliefs that are inconsistent with the relationship or counterconformity—challenging the group by consistently expressing alternative beliefs and actions. As a form of pressure, it affects a leader as suggested by institutional theory (Oliver, 1991). Nonconformity, the tendency to act contrary to prevailing standards, attitudes, and practices of relationships, is a mechanism that is predicated on power or asymmetric interaction (Cialdini, 1984).

5.2 Theories of Strategic Interaction

5.2.1 *Agency Theory*

Agency theory (Jensen & Meckling, 1976; Alchian & Demsetz, 1972) proposes that a principal uses an agent to fairly represent his or her interest. Through control and incentives, the principal aligns the interest of the agent with his or her interest by using legal mechanisms mostly but sometimes social influence. What keeps the relationship functional is the transparency required of the agent: the latter has to always represent the interest of the principal as fairly as possible to sustain the relationship. In the context of followership, the principal is the leader while the follower, in his or her role as agent, acts transparently to sustain the relationship consistent with the interests of both parties. To the extent that strategic followers strive to maximize outcomes for the relational constituents, they function as agents.

Strategic Interactions   95

The application of agency theory to strategic followership seems fairly easy for three main reasons. First, the principal–agent relationship is similar or identical to the leader–followership relationship. The power of the principal and leader affects the agent and follower. There is also control and alignment of interests even though the enforcement mechanisms sometimes differ. Unlike the principal, who can use legal mechanisms to enforce compliance, the leader often has to rely on social mechanisms to enforce compliance. To the extent that the leader is bad, the follower has the moral basis to deny compliance with nonlegal consequences. In contrast, the noncompliance of the agent can be redressed by a principal who is behaving badly (Holloway & van Rhyn, 2005). Second, both relationships involve optimization of mutual interest. The principal, through incentive alignment, seeks to maximize the interest of the agent so that the latter, in turn, will maximize the principal's interest. Of course, it sometimes does not work particularly when there are aberrations such as greediness of the agent who seeks excess rewards or the principal is stingy and does not want to fairly reward the agent. The leader can also align his interest with that of the follower through a combination of pecuniary and nonpecuniary reward systems. Third, both relationships function with similar dynamics, mechanisms, and processes. They involve interaction, the use of power and control, and change as a function of situations, personal attributes, and relational characteristics. In the context of strategic followership and strategic leadership, both have a strategic element in that they involve stratagem (conduits of influence) and strategic outcomes (Ireland & Hitt, 1999; Zoogah, 2014).

A number of agency roles are also followership roles. A realtor, in representing the interest of the seller or buyer as principal, functions as a follower. To the extent that the interests of the realtor and buyer or seller are aligned, outcomes that maximize their interests are likely to be achieved. Within organizations, directors or executives function as agents. Corporate governance theory (see Baker & Anderson, 2010) suggests that the board of directors is to oversee the actions of the director who is an agent for the shareholders. To the extent that the director represents the interests of the owners of the organization, he or she is likely to make decisions and take strategic actions that yield greater value for shareholders (Eisenhardt, 1989). A followership lens can thus be applied to the director to understand the nomological network of factors shaping his strategic behavior and either facilitating or constraining the expected outcomes.

5.2.2 Exchange Theory

Exchange theory, particularly social exchange, has been overwhelmingly used in the micro field of organizational behavior and leadership (see leader–member exchange—LMX theory and organizational justice and trust theories). The macro equivalent—economic exchange theory—however, has

96　*Strategic Interactions*

not received equivalent treatment. Economic exchange focuses on transactions with economic units (Williamson, 1975, 1985). In those economic exchanges one party is a buyer and the other a seller. Each plays a different role. Just as middle managers function as both followers of higher level managers and leaders of lower level subordinates (Uhl-Bien, Riggio, Lowe, & Carsten, 2014), one organization that is a buyer of raw materials from a supplier also serves as a supplier of products to customers. The organization can thus function as a strategic follower by enacting restorative and transcendent behaviors that increase the value to constituents of both following and leading organizations (Sharapov & Ross, 2015). Economic exchange theory that specifies buyer and seller roles is more suitable for the interactional perspective of strategic followership which operates at the organizational level. It does not, however, preclude application to the psychological perspective or interpersonal level. To the extent that a follower is viewed as 'selling' innovative ideas to the leader who 'buys' them, an economic exchange perspective can be applied. Consultants who 'sell' ideas on organizational development and strategic advance to chief executive officers exemplify this application.

5.2.3 Political Theory

Political theory has been applied to organizations in the form of organizational politics because of the recognition that political behavior is an inevitable part of organizational life. Organizational politics refers to the "actions by individuals which are directed toward the goal of furthering their own self-interests without regard for the well-being of others or their organization" (Kacmar & Baron, 1999: 4). Others define it as the process by which an individual employee uses an informal network to gain power and accomplish tasks to meet his or her wants or needs (Pfeffer, 1981) or behaviors that are designed to foster self-interest and are taken without regard to or at the expense of organizational goals (Mintzberg, 1983, 1985; Witt, Andrews, & Kacmar, 2000). It is now generally agreed that even though organizational politics tends to be negative when people promote self-interest, it can also be a positive practice when the greater good of the company is affected. It is for the latter perspective that I consider it as part of strategic followership. Recall that strategic followership is positively valenced (Zoogah, 2014). From that perspective, a follower who functions as a representative of a department in cross-departmental interactions or activities has a constituency to which he or she has to report. In that capacity, the follower presents the constituency in a positive way through the acquisition of scarce resources, maintenance, or an enhancement of image. By examining the political behavior of followers, researchers are likely to discern the representation role of followers. Indeed, the effectiveness of that role can be examined to draw insight for managers.

5.2.4 Tournament Theory

Tournament theory emerged from personnel economics. It is used to describe situations where wage differences are based not on marginal productivity but instead on relative differences between the individuals (Lazear & Rosen, 1981). Prototypic studies include Holmstrom (1982), Carmichael (1983), Rosen (1986), and Lazear (1989). Basically, a tournament is a situation where a group of employees of a certain rank in an organization compete for promotion to the next level of the job hierarchy, with the promotion (and associated wage increase) awarded to the employee with the highest performance. The employer chooses the tournament prize which is the difference in wages between the post-promotion and pre-promotion jobs. Typically, the employer selects a prize that would induce the optimal level of worker effort. The optimality of the effort level refers to the effort level that maximizes the firm's profit. The employer does not want to choose a wage spread that is too small because it will not induce employees to compete for promotion, and as a result they may invest too little effort, which leads to lower levels of employee performance and ultimately lower levels of firm performance. On the other hand, if the employee sets a wage spread that is too high it may become detrimental to the firm.

Tournaments are in professional sports, law practice, professional writing, politics, innovation, and so on (see Connelly, Tihany, Crook, & Gangloff, 2014). The theory can be applied to strategic followership to optimize the strategic behavior of followers. To what extent do supervisors with multiple subordinates use tournament to optimize outcomes? Supervisors can design relational tournaments, reward followers on differential outcomes attained as a result of relational activities. Even though tournament theory presupposes rational actors who seek to maximize individual utility (Connelly, Tihanyi, Crook, & Gangloff, 2014), followers are rational to the extent that they seek the 'betterment' of their organizations and want to contribute value to it. They assume collective utility in place of individual utility because of their transcendent selves or desire for the collective good. Tournament theory is also likely to induce a context for maximizing collective rather than individual good. Strategic followers are presumed to be willing and able to act but may be constrained by the readiness of the leader to facilitate their contributions. To the extent that the leader assembles followers with the same mindset (i.e., strategic orientations), the size of the tournament that is determined by both the number of unique competitors (termed the breath), and the number of possible levels (termed the depth) can induce strategic followers to optimize their contributions. Of course, leadership and followership are based on influence (i.e., cooperative mechanisms) and therefore seem contrary to competition. Nevertheless, competition from a stress perspective challenges the potential of individuals and groups.

98 *Strategic Interactions*

Given that positive stress (i.e., eustress) leads to optimal outcomes (Cavanaugh, Boswell, Roehling, & Boudreau, 2000; Lazarus & Folkman, 1984; Yerkes & Dodson, 1908), healthy competition, as suggested by tournament theory, can yield extraordinary outcomes for leaders and organizations. I recognize that a strategic follower's likelihood of winning depends on the effort expended; irreducible random components, such as leadership changes, organizational crisis, and biases of leaders; and mechanisms that facilitate or constrain the tournament. Nevertheless, the theory can help us understand the interactions of followers with leaders. It may also help us understand the value curve of strategic followership (Zoogah, 2014). Continued compensation for leaders' bad behaviors is only beneficial to a certain point after which it becomes too costly to the follower to motivate him- or herself to higher levels of performance, and strategic follower effectiveness declines if the follower puts pressure on him- or herself. As a result, restorative behavior may have an inverted-U-shape relationship based on tournament theory.

5.2.5 Signaling Theory

One assumption of strategic followership is that leaders are ready to enable followers' contributions. Leaders may thus signal their readiness by sending messages formally or informally, directly or indirectly, sporadically or frequently to followers about not only the type but also the frequency and level of contribution desired. Leaders of a young firm in an initial public offering, for example, may stack their board with a diverse group of prestigious directors to send a message to potential investors (followers) about the firm's legitimacy (Certo, 2003; Filatotchev & Bishop, 2002). Signaling theory fundamentally focuses on reducing information asymmetry between two parties (Spence, 2002). Spence's (1973) seminal work on labor markets demonstrated how a job applicant might engage in behaviors to reduce information asymmetry that hampers the selection ability of prospective employers. Spence illustrated how high-quality prospective employees distinguish themselves from low-quality prospects via the costly signal of rigorous higher education. Since then there has been a large volume of studies using signaling theory across a range of disciplines from anthropology to zoology (Bliege-Bird & Smith, 2005). In the management field, studies in strategy show how CEOs signal the unobservable quality of their firms to potential investors via the observable quality of their financial statements (Zhang & Wiersema, 2009). Others show how firms use heterogeneous boards to communicate adherence to social values to a range of organizational stakeholders (Miller & del Carmen Triana, 2009). A third group examines the signaling value of board characteristics (Certo, 2003), top management team characteristics (Lester, Certo, Dalton, Dalton, & Cannella, 2006), venture capitalist and angel investor presence (Elitzur & Gavious, 2003), founder involvement (Busenitz, Fiet, & Moesel, 2005), and human resource management (Suazo, Martínez, & Sandoval, 2009).

In the leadership and followership literature, very few, if any, studies have actually used signaling theory to investigate the exchanges. Of course, there have been suggestions and anecdotal evidence of signals in the influence process. For example, Price and van Vugt (2014) suggest that "the opportunity to lead a hunt might afford one an opportunity to show off attractive traits such as hunting skill, health, and formidability" and "this advertising could lead to fitness-enhancing social and mating opportunities that would compensate the leader for leadership costs" (p. 11) because costly signaling theory proposes that acts of providing public goods to one's group can serve as a valuable opportunity to advertise one's desirable qualities to potential allies, cooperative partners, and mates (Gintis, Smith, & Bowles, 2001; Hawkes & Bliege-Bird, 2002).

The components of signaling theory—information asymmetry and the signaling environment, which comprises the signaler, the signal, the receiver, and feedback (Connelly et al., 2014)—apply to strategic followership. The potential contribution of a strategic follower is information that is asymmetric to the follower and the leader. As a result, signals can be exchanged about this contribution. The behaviors of the signaler and receiver, as well as feedback between them, can also be investigated to understand why the contribution of a follower is either lower than or greater than expected. In addition, the nature and transmission of the signal might be investigated to improve insight into strategic followership. For example, signals for when the restorative action of followers can begin are likely to enhance understanding of the restorative value generated by a strategic follower. Price and van Vugt (2014) suggest that disrespectful followers of beneficial leaders will attract social penalties (punishment and/or social exclusion) from other followers, whereas disrespectful followers of nonbeneficial leaders will attract social rewards (enhanced reputation and prestige) from other followers. Because social penalties blunt future contributions, it is important to know what signals a strategic follower can provide to enable him or her to contribute value without incurring social penalties. What signals are effective in private (only follower–leader interface) or public (follower–organization interface) is also an interesting question to be explored. Answers to this and similar questions will contribute to the literature on the emerging domain.

Summary

In sum, the strategic interactions of a follower with a leader vary as a function of the dependency orientation of the firms. The influence dynamics depend on the perception of superiority manifested in the orientations. In

100 *Strategic Interactions*

equal orientations, the influence dynamics are similar. However, in unequal orientations, the dynamics are dissimilar and affect the cognitive and behavioral tendencies of followers and leaders. This view is supported by resource-dependence theory (Pfeffer & Salancik, 1978; Hillman, Withers, & Collins, 2009; Oliver, 1991). The political theory literature also suggests that the role of a politician depends on the level of dependency on the constituencies (Schuler, Rehbein, & Cramer, 2001). Third, stakeholder theory (Freeman, 1984) contends that the behavior of organizations toward stakeholders is determined by the degree of dependence for resources. Theories of symbolism, routines, and networks also suggest that the experience of the follower with the leader is likely to be determined by the particular orientation. Symmetric orientations are likely to lead to meaningful or flourishing experiences while asymmetric orientations may not because of the position—inferior or superior—of each firm and/or individual during the interaction.

5.3 Strategic Cognition

Cognition, the mental process of acquiring knowledge and understanding through thought, experience, and the senses, is a major factor in strategic interactions because of the judgment and decision processes that are central to strategic followership. In other words, cognition has strategic components that influence interactions of followers. Information possessed by a follower can be used to manipulate (in a positive sense) the behavioral responses of a leader. Consequently, strategic cognition theories are appropriate for strategic interactions.

The cognitive school of strategic management shows that strategy formation is a mental process (Mintzberg, Ahlstrand, & Lampel, 1998). Both the *positivistic* view, which "treats the processing and structuring of knowledge as an effort to produce some kind of objective motion picture of the world," and the *constructivist* view, which contends that strategy is some kind of interpretation of the events, the symbols, the behavior of customer, or the world of the organization (Mintzberg, Ahlstrand, & Lampel, 1998: 155), suggest that cognitive bias or the mental limitations of the strategist, as well as information processing of managers and organizations, and the configuration of structures of knowledge by the mind influence interactions in varied ways. The cognitive school of strategic management thus suggests several theories of relevance to strategic followership: strategic cognition, strategic mental models, information theory, and competence theory. These are cognitive representations or scripts that orient the behavior of individuals during interactions toward fundamental individual, group, and organizational outcomes. Such theories may help us to understand the mind-set of strategic followers in their relations with leaders. Psychological capital theory, which focuses on the degree to which individuals possess psychological resources of hope, efficacy, resilience, and optimism, which maximizes their performance, can also be used to understand the strategic interactions.

5.3.1 Strategic Cognition Theory

Strategic cognition, the locus of which is mind-sets or knowledge structures of followers and leaders as individuals or organizations, is particularly important in strategic decision-making (Dean & Sharfman, 1996; Mintzberg, Raisinghani, & Theoret, 1976). For organizational agents, there is evidence from strategic cognition research that organizational strategies result from *strategic consensus*, defined as the process by which organizations reach consensus on desired strategies and outcomes (Walsh, 1995), *managerial cognition*, the process by which cognitions of managers influence their orientation to strategic systems of organizations (Walsh, 1995), and *organizational cognition*, the process by which cognitive systems of organizations impact systems and operations of organizations (Hodgkinson & Healey, 2008; Mintzberg et al., 1998). Together they show that cognitive structures of individual managers, teams, organizations, and industries influence interactions of individuals and operations of organizations (Mintzberg et al., 1998).

The mind-sets of leading and follower organizations, for example, otherwise termed mental models or mental maps (Barr, Stimpert, & Huff, 1992), have been shown to be significant drivers of knowledge capture and knowledge sharing (Lyles & Schwenk, 1992). In their comparative study of two railroads, Rock Island and C&NW, over a twenty-five-year period, Barr et al. (1992) found the organizations were similar, to begin with, but one eventually went bankrupt while the other survived probably because of differential strategic cognitions of the respective managers (i.e., the causal maps about the railway industry environment). Even though both organizations ascribed poor performance to bad weather, government programs, and regulations, one organization's maps shifted to a focus on the relationships between costs, productivity, and management style that resulted in performance changes. The latter achieved different outcomes because of discernment of the situation and engaged in different strategic behaviors that yielded superior outcomes.

5.3.2 Information Processing Theory

The information processing view suggests that followers are information workers by acquiring, sharing or distributing information within the organizational system. They facilitate operations through attention, encoding, storage and retrieval, choice, and assessment of outcomes (Corner, Kinicki, & Keats, 1994; Mintzberg et al., 1998). First, attention (i.e., the observation by the follower) determines what information he or she processes and what is ignored. Second, the follower encodes it in

102 *Strategic Interactions*

relation to some acquired standard (expected behavior). The encoding ensures that the desire meaning, which comes about through looking for a fit between the information and existing categories (e.g., praise instead of condemnation), is achieved by the follower. Third, the follower stores the information in memory, the web of associations between different items of information so that it can be accessed later. For organizations, "the associations are also embodied in forms, rules, procedures, conventions, and technologies" (Mintzberg et al., 1998: 161). The fourth step is choice. Choice of the process of selecting an option that fulfills a strategic need is iterative which culminates in a resolution. Because it is an iterative process, choice changes based on information from internal and external sources of followers. The change is a function of the interaction. Last, there is an assessment of the outcomes. As Mintzberg et al. (1998) indicate, the outcomes herald the beginning of the feedback process whereby individuals and organizations make sense of their choices. It is this last step that is crucial because the follower assesses the degree to which the observation that is encoded is congruent with the value criterions either by organizational or personal agency.

5.3.3 *Strategic Mental Model Theory*

Mental models refer to 'deeply ingrained assumptions, generalizations, or even pictures and images that influence how we understand the world and how we take action' (Senge, 1990: 8, citing Gardner, 1985). A mental model consists of three major components: key variables, causal mechanisms that connect the variables, and the overall structure and boundaries of the system as envisioned by the model's owner (Sterman, 2000). As organized knowledge structures that allow strategic followers to interact with their relational environment, mental models allow followers and leaders "to predict and explain the behavior of the world around them, to recognize and remember relationships among components of the environment, and to construct expectations for what is likely to occur next" (Mathieu et al., 2000: 274). Furthermore, mental models allow people to draw inferences, make predictions, understand phenomena, decide which actions to take, and experience events vicariously (Johnson-Laird, 1983). Rouse and Morris (1986) define a mental model as a "mechanism whereby humans generate descriptions of system purpose and form, explanations of system functioning and observed system states, and predictions of future system states" (p. 360). Thus, mental models help individuals to describe, explain, and predict events in their environment. In other words, it determines their interactions.

Applied to strategic followership, a mental model is the cognitive representation of a strategic followership role. It is strategic to the extent that the envisioned role is linked to—value creation and other outcomes of constituents in the relationship. What elements and what connections among them are perceived most important are partially determined by the followers and partially by leaders of the strategic follower. Even though the mental model is held by the strategic follower, its enactment results in a judgment of its efficacy by the leader. The convergence of enactment and judgment is a manifestation of a shared mental model, the degree to which the leader and follower have a common understanding about the particular issue, event, activity, problem, solution, or strategy. Shared mental models may focus on the task (procedures, expectations, and contingencies), technology (ideals, likely failures), interactions (roles/responsibilities, information sources, interaction patterns, communication channels, role interdependencies, information flow), and exchange members (knowledge, skills, attitudes, preferences) (Mathieu et al., 2000).

In a study exploring the mental models of competitive strategists, Hodgkinson and Johnson (1994) argue that studies are "predicated on the assumption that there are high levels of consensus within and between organizations in a given industry concerning the bases of competition and the positioning of particular organizations" and examine "the mental models of individuals in order to examine empirically the nature and extent of such consensus" (p. 525). They interviewed twenty-three managers from two organizations in the UK grocery retailing industry. They found considerable variation in the nature of the cognitive categories elicited from the participants, the overall complexity of their taxonomies on competitive structures, both within and between the organizations. Similarly, strategic followers and leaders may have different models (i.e., worldviews) on value creation. In bad leadership contexts, such models may underlie the value diminishing behaviors of bad leaders and value restoration behaviors of strategic followers. Strategic shared mental models, organized knowledge structures that allow followers and leaders to interact with each other in a way that enables them to predict and explain the behavior of each other and to construct expectations for strategic outcomes for relational constituents, are therefore important in understanding strategic interactions.

5.3.4 Competence Theory

One major element of strategic cognition is knowledge, a view highlighted by competence theory. It not only crosses levels from individual (personal competence) to groups (team competence) and organizations (organizational competence). It has behavioral, affective, and cognitive forms. The latter focuses on knowledge. Since Penrose (1959), who advanced the competence of organizations, the knowledge-based perspective of firm competence, for example, has gained greater prominence and strategic implications. Spender (1994), for example, argued that cognitive attributes of managers (i.e., managerial cognition) facilitate decision-making, which enables organizations to gain a competitive advantage.

104 *Strategic Interactions*

Leaders, as managers, have knowledge that has strategic value (Spender, 1994). Consequently, how they behave or use their knowledge can negatively affect that strategic value. The restorative dimension of strategic followership proposes that followers take action to restore the resultant value diminishment. A restorative follower discerns the competence (strategic cognition) of the leader (Kellerman, 2004, 2008) as a basis for taking restorative action. Research on competence as a strategic cognition can therefore focus on the response of followers to leader competence or strategic knowledge. At the moment, there is little research on how strategic cognition from the competence perspective drives followers to engage in restorative and/or transcendent actions.

5.2.5 Psychological Capital Theory

There is growing evidence that competitive advantage of organizations does not depend solely on traditional economic and human capital but also on social capital and more recently psychological capital (Luthans, Luthans, & Luthans, 2004). Psychological capital refers to the positive and developmental state of an individual as characterized by high self-efficacy, hope, optimism, and resiliency (SHOR; Luthans Youssef, & Avolio, 2007). As an attribute of identity—"who you are" (Luthans et al., 2004), psychological capital involves awareness of one's capacities to interact, work, and achieve certain outcomes. The four elements—SHOR—are cognitive attributes that capacitate an individual.

In the context of strategic followership, the capacities are important particularly in restorative followership situations. A follower seeking to restore diminished value has to first assess his or her (1) conviction, (2) abilities to mobilize the resources, and (3) courses of action needed to successfully enact behavior that can restore diminished value. Given the likelihood of social and organizational constraints, these self-efficacy beliefs are not only significant, but they must also be followed by "a positive motivational state that is based on an interactively derived sense of successful (a) agency (goal-oriented energy) and (b) pathways (planning to meet goals)" (Snyder, Irving, & Anderson, 1991: p. 289). In other words, the person must have hope about the specific outcomes (e.g., how much value to be restored). The disposition or tendency to look on the more favorable side of events or conditions and to expect the most favorable outcome (i.e., optimism) is essential because of the potential for things to go bad. The follower might be undermined, face social opprobrium, or be victimized. When restorative actions either do not yield the desired outcomes (i.e., failure to restore diminished value), resilience is needed to initiate subsequent action. Resilience refers to the capacity to recover quickly from difficulties. Coutu (2002) indicates that resilient people have (a) a staunch acceptance of reality; (b) a deep belief, often buttressed by strongly held values, that life is meaningful;

and (c) an uncanny ability to improvise and adapt to significant change. Restorative followers with these attributes are more likely to persist in their restorative efforts.

Of course, as a capacity, psychological capital can be developed. Followers who lack or are deficient in these capacities can develop them. Luthans et al. (2004) suggest four ways by which psychological capital can be developed: mastery experiences or performance attainments, vicarious experiences or modeling, social persuasion, and physiological and psychological arousal. Successful restorative actions in a particular context empower the individual in subsequent situations. Followers who observe others effectively transcend followership situations can leverage the insight from that in other contexts. Effective social dissuasions and repeated or determined efforts enable a follower to achieve resiliency.

Psychological capital presents an opportunity for research particularly via the "mediated and/or direct routes" of strategic followership. The effect of self-efficacy on strategic outcomes of followers can be examined to determine how psychological capital influence strategic followership. Resiliency in the face of bad leadership or social and organizational constraints can also be examined in much the same way that hope and optimism can be used to examine transcendent followership.

In sum, the degree to which individuals possess psychological resources of hope, efficacy, resilience, and optimism, can be used to understand the two paths—mediated and direct—of strategic followership. Psychological resources such as SHOR are essential for the journey given the thorns that bestrew the path of followership.

5.4 Strategic Affect

Follower–leader exchanges involve affective processes that determine relational and organizational outcomes. Strategic affect focuses on affective reactions of followers that influence strategic objectives of parties in the relational interface. Strategic affect is contextual; it antecedes the strategic decisions and behaviors of followers in restorative and transcendent followership. Before discussing its role, it is important to explain what I mean by affect. The definition of *affect* depends on the literature of interest—neuroscience or psychology. The literature of neuroscientists and medical professionals including neuroimaging, neuroanatomy or neurocircuitry, who usually take a pragmatic view (e.g., Carmona, Holland, & Harrison, 2009; Etkin & Wager, 2007; Ruby & Decety, 2004; Vogt, 2005), often see affect as similar to the everyday use of the label (LeDoux, 2000). Affect is thus emotion. In the psychology and management literature, affect is regarded as a superordinate concept that incorporates the concepts of feeling, emotion, and mood (Barsade & Gibson, 2007; Van Kleef, De Dreu, & Manstead, 2006; Schwarz & Clore, 2007).

106 *Strategic Interactions*

While feeling is understood as the conscious and subjective experience of emotions (Johnston, 2003; Ortony & Clore, 1989; Zajonc, 1980), mood is an affective state that is global and diffuse (free floating), likely to be outside awareness, and not connected to any single object (Barsade & Gibson, 2007). Emotion, the most complex of these affective concepts, is an object-specific, intense affective state that is short-lived (Barsade & Gibson, 2007; Brief & Weiss, 2002; Davis, 2009). The definition suggests that a follower's response to bad or good leadership might depend on the affective state of that person. Besides that, the knowledge associated with affects can inform not only the response but also the decisions of followers in strategic situations.

Even though affect as information and affect-induced cognitive processing are important psychologically (Gasper & Zawadzki, 2013; Schwarz, 2012), it is the strategic implications of affective knowledge that is germane in strategic followership. Affective knowledge refers to knowledge where affect extensively reduces causal ambiguity. In uncertain or risky situations, affect may take on the role to reduce this uncertainty by recalculating "cold" mental probabilities of what a follower knows to date relevant to the current issue, as well as possible actions for improving the situation. Here, affect's role is to increase the confidence in relevant knowledge by reducing the felt uncertainty. This can lead to bad or good practices and strategic actions in relation to the particular strategic situation, since the role of affect is not to solve the situation, but to enhance the sense of being closer to an ontological reality. Even though all knowledge is affective to a certain extent (Bower, 1981), for affective knowledge, affect is particularly strong enough to extensively alter the mental probability calculations away from "cold" thinking. Given that affect is intertwined with cognition (Duncan & Barrett, 2007), it follows that affect is involved in transferring information into practice and knowledge. Knowledge conversion—that is, the transfer of experience from one individual to another (Argote & Ingram, 2000)—is a main mechanism creating practices on the individual level as well as upward to the organizational level through social interaction among other followers (Miron-Spektor, Gino, & Argote, 2011; Nonaka & Takeuchi, 1995).

Affective knowledge therefore plays a major role in strategic followership. First, it antecedes decisions and actions of followers. Second, it reinforces or strengthens chosen plans and actions. Third, it validates or justifies adopted plans or behaviors. Last, it enables followers to connect with other followers in the acquisition, processing, and development of affect-based knowledge.

5.4.1 Strategic Trust

One affect-centered factor in strategic followership is trust (i.e., strategic trust). Strategic trust is fundamental to organizational outcomes.

While some scholars refer to it as the trust employees have in executives to make the right strategic decisions (Hoe, 2007) others apply it in the context of morality as moral commitment to treat employees as if they were trustworthy (Uslaner, 2002). I refer to it as the degree to which a follower believes in the goodwill of relational constituents to act with integrity in the execution of their strategic roles. It combines moralistic trust, which based on "some sort of belief in the goodwill of the other" (Seligman, 1997: 43; Yamagishi & Yamagishi, 1994: 131), or altruistic trust (Mansbridge, 1999), and transcendent trust, the belief in the reliability of the leader to overcome challenges to fulfill strategic roles. Transcendent trust is not used religiously here but consistent with transcendent virtues.

How does strategic trust relate to strategic followership? Because followership is an exchange, both focus on the strategic component of beliefs and roles, respectively. Second, they are oriented toward the leader. The first view of strategic trust, which centers on bad leadership, is based on the expectation or belief that the bad leader will not behave in a way that diminishes value. The second view has a similar expectation, but the value generated by the leader is optimal. How it drives the restorative and transcendent behavior of followers in bad and good leadership contexts, respectively, needs to be investigated for us to appreciate the role of affect in strategic followership. Affect is not behavior. As a result, strategic affect influences the behavior of strategic followers through signals. In other words, the likes and dislikes of followers for a leader's behavior signal the former's likely action. Consequently, signaling theory, which is useful for describing behavior when two parties have access to different information (Bliege-Bird & Smith, 2005), can be used to understand how strategic affect influence strategic followership. As I discussed in previous chapters, signals from strategic followers communicate the likely behavioral responses while those from leaders communicate the acceptance or endorsement of followers' reactions. The convergence of those signals may trigger action or strategic response. Strategic followership research can benefit from studies that examine this convergence.

5.4.2 Social Exchange Theory

Within this framework is positive affect manifested in what is generally called emotional intelligence which has been studied extensively (see Goleman, 1995; Zeidner, Matthews, & Roberts, 2004 for a review of emotional intelligence in the workplace). A growing body of research shows that investing in EI creates more engaged, committed employees and customers. EI has been shown to (1) foster collaborative and agile teams, (2) build stronger connections with customers, and (3) make companies more profitable. At the interpersonal level, Schutte et al. (2001) found

108 *Strategic Interactions*

that EI is associated with empathy, perspective taking, self-monitoring in social situations, cooperativeness toward partners, close and affectionate relations, and greater satisfaction in relationships. Gardner and Stough (2002: 74) also found "a strong relationship between transformational leadership and overall emotional intelligence" because leaders who use transformational behaviors motivate their employees to do more than is expected (Yammarino, Spangler, & Bass, 1993). The components of EI—*self-awareness* which refers to the ability to understand feelings and accurate self-assessment; *self-management*, defined as the ability to manage internal states, impulses and resources; *social awareness*, the ability to read people and groups accurately; and *relationship management*, the ability to induce desirable responses in others (Goleman, 2001: 27)— are relationship-dependent. In other words, competence influences and is influenced by the relational context. It can thus determine acquisition of relational capital because the competencies of the individual facilitate response to the social or relational cues.

Followers who are emotionally intelligent are self-aware, manage their internal states and resources, read social cues effectively, and induce desirable responses from both bad and good leaders. They are also able to devise strategies that seem consistent with the relational environment in a way that yields positive outcomes. Furthermore, positive affect enables strategic followers not only to exploit opportunities in the relational context but also to parry away constraints. Understanding the strategies of such followers and the outcomes from positive and negative affect can increase understanding of how strategic followers contribute to the strategic objectives of organizations by facilitating achievement of relational capital through the use of affective competencies.

In conclusion, strategic affect, defined as the degree to which positive affective states facilitate strategic outcomes, revolves around emotional competence. Broadly, it refers to positive and negative affect. However, given the destructive effects of the latter, it is more likely the ability to overcome negative affect (a function of emotional intelligence) that contributes to strategic outcomes. With regard to their contribution to the relationship positive affect can be leveraged in restorative and transcendent situations when followers need to influence bad and good leaders, respectively.

Note

1. In Physics an interaction refers to the transfer of energy between elementary particles.

References

Adler, P. S., & Kwon, S. W. (2000). Social capital: The good, the bad, and the ugly. In Lesser, E. (Ed.), *Knowledge and Social Capital: Foundations and Applications* (pp. 89–115). Boston: Butterworth-Heinemann.

Afzal, W. (2015). Towards the general theory of information asymmetry. In M. M. Al-Suqri & A. S. AlAufi (Eds.), *Information Seeking Behavior and Technology Adoption: Theories and Trends* (pp. 124–135). Hershey, PA: IGI Global.

Alchian, A. A., & Demsetz, H. (1972). Production, information costs, and economic organization. *The American Economic Review*, 62(5), 777–795.

Akerlof, G. (1970). The market for lemons: Qualitative uncertainty and the market mechanism. *Quarterly Journal of Economics*, 84(3).

Argote, L., & Ingram, P. (2000). Knowledge transfer: A basis for competitive advantage in firms. *Organizational Behavior and Human Decision Processes*, 82(1), 150–169.

Baker, H. K., & Anderson, R. (2010). *Corporate Governance: A Synthesis of Theory, Research, and Practice*. New Jersey: John Wiley & Sons.

Barling, J. (2014). *The Science of Leadership: Lessons from Research for Organizational Leaders*. Oxford, New York: Oxford University Press.

Barr, P. S., Stimpert, J. L., & Huff, A. S. (1992). Cognitive change, strategic action, and organizational renewal. *Strategic Management Journal*, 13(S1), 15–36.

Barsade, S. G., & Gibson, D. E. (2007). Why does affect matter in organizations? *Academy of Management Perspectives*, 21(1), 36–59.

Bliege-Bird, R., & Smith, E. (2005). Signaling theory, strategic interaction, and symbolic capital. *Current Anthropology*, 46(2), 221–248.

Bower, G. H. (1981). Mood and memory. *American Psychologist*, 36(2), 129.

Boyle, B. A., & Dwyer, F. R. (1995). Power, bureaucracy, influence, and performance: Their relationships in industrial distribution channels. *Journal of Business Research*, 32(3), 189–200.

Brief, A. P., & Weiss, H. M. (2002). Organizational behavior: Affect in the workplace. *Annual Review of Psychology*, 53(1), 279–307.

Brodbeck, F. C., Kerschreiter, R., Mojzisch, A., & Schulz-Hardt, S. (2007). Group decision making under conditions of distributed knowledge: The information asymmetries model. *Academy of Management Review*, 32(2), 459–479.

Busenitz, L. W., Fiet, J. O., & Moesel, D. D. (2005). Signaling in venture capitalist—New venture team funding decisions: Does it indicate long–term venture outcomes? *Entrepreneurship Theory and Practice*, 29(1), 1–12.

Cable, D. M., & Judge, T. A. (2003). Managers' upward influence tactic strategies: The role of manager personality and supervisor leadership style. *Journal of Organizational Behavior: The International Journal of Industrial, Occupational and Organizational Psychology and Behavior*, 24(2), 197–214.

Camerer, C. F., & Weber, R. (2013). Experimental organizational economics. In R. Gibbons & J. Roberts (Eds.), *The Handbook of Organizational Economics* (pp. 213–262). Princeton, NJ: Princeton University Press

Capron, L., & Shen, J. C. (2007). Acquisitions of private vs. public firms: Private information, target selection, and acquirer returns. *Strategic Management Journal*, 28(9), 891–911.

Carmona, J. E., Holland, A. K., & Harrison, D. W. (2009). Extending the functional cerebral systems theory of emotion to the vestibular modality: A systematic and integrative approach. *Psychological Bulletin*, 135(2), 286.

Carmichael, H. L. (1983). The agent-agents problem: Payment by relative output. *Journal of Labor Economics*, 1(1), 50–65.

Casciaro, T., & Piskorski, M. J. (2005). Power imbalance, mutual dependence, and constraint absorption: A closer look at resource dependence theory. *Administrative Science Quarterly*, 50(2), 167–199.

110 *Strategic Interactions*

Cavanaugh, M. A., Boswell, W. R., Roehling, M. V., & Boudreau, J. W. (2000). An empirical examination of self-reported work stress among US managers. *Journal of Applied Psychology*, 85(1), 65.

Certo, S. T. (2003). Influencing initial public offering investors with prestige: Signaling with board structures. *Academy of Management Review*, 28(3), 432–446.

Cialdini, R. B. (1984). *Influence: How and Why People Agree to Things*. New York: Quill.

Cialdini, R. (1993). *The Psychology of Influence*. New York: William Morrow & Co.

Cohen, B. D., & Dean, T. J. (2005). Information asymmetry and investor valuation of IPOs: Top management team legitimacy as a capital market signal. *Strategic Management Journal*, 26(7), 683–690.

Coleman, James S. (1990). *Foundations of Social Theory*. Cambridge, MA: Belknap Press.

Connelly, B. L., Tihanyi, L., Crook, T. R., & Gangloff, K. A. (2014). Tournament Theory: Thirty Years of Contests and Competitions. *Journal of Management*, 40(1), 16–47

Corner, P. D., Kinicki, A. J., & Keats, B. W. (1994). Integrating organizational and individual information processing perspectives on choice. *Organization Science*, 5(3), 294–308.

Coutu, D. L. (2002). How resilience works. *Harvard Business Review*, 80(5), 46–56.

Davis, M. A. (2009). Understanding the relationship between mood and creativity: A meta-analysis. *Organizational Behavior and Human Decision Processes*, 108(1), 25–38.

Dean Jr, J. W., & Sharfman, M. P. (1996). Does decision process matter? A study of strategic decision-making effectiveness. *Academy of Management Journal*, 39(2), 368–392.

Dooley, R. S., & Fryxell, G. E. (1999). Attaining decision quality and commitment from dissent: The moderating effects of loyalty and competence in strategic decision-making teams. *Academy of Management Journal*, 42(4), 389–402.

Duncan, S., & Barrett, L. F. (2007). Affect is a form of cognition: A neurobiological analysis. *Cognition and Emotion*, 21(6), 1184–1211.

Elitzur, R., & Gavious, A. 2003. Contracting, signaling, and moral hazard: A model of entrepreneurs, "angels," and venture capitalists. *Journal of Business Venturing*, 18, 709–725.

Eisenhardt, K. M. (1989). Agency theory: An assessment and review. *Academy of Management Review*, 14(1), 57–74.

Etkin, A., & Wager, T. D. (2007). Functional neuroimaging of anxiety: A meta-analysis of emotional processing in PTSD, social anxiety disorder, and specific phobia. *American Journal of Psychiatry*, 164(10), 1476–1488.

Etzioni, A. (1975). *A Comparative Analysis of Complex Organizations*. New York: Free PressSimon and Schuster.

Finkelstein, S., Hambrick, D. C., & Cannella, A. A. (2009). *Strategic Leadership: Theory and Research on Executives, Top Management Teams, and Boards*. New York: Oxford University Press.

Filatotchev, I., & Bishop, K. (2002). Board composition, share ownership, and 'underpricing'of UK IPO firms. *Strategic Management Journal*, 23(10), 941–955.

Frazier, G. L., & Rody, R. C. (1991). The use of influence strategies in interfirm relationships in industrial product channels. *The Journal of Marketing*, 52–69.

Frazier, G. L., & Summers, J. O. (1984). Interfirm influence strategies and their application within distribution channels. *The Journal of Marketing*, 43–55.

Frazier, G. L., & Summers, J. O. (1986). Perceptions of interfirm power and its use within a franchise channel of distribution. *Journal of Marketing Research*, 169–176.

Freeman, R. E. (1984). *Strategic Management: A Stakeholder Approach*. Boston: Pitman.

French, J. R., Raven, B., & Cartwright, D. (1959). The bases of social power. *Classics of Organization Theory*, 7, 311–320.

Galaskiewicz, J. (1985). Interorganizational relations. *Annual Review of Sociology*, 11(1), 281–304.

Garcés-Ayerbe, C., Rivera-Torres, P., & Murillo-Luna, J. L. (2012). Stakeholder pressure and environmental proactivity: Moderating effect of competitive advantage expectations. *Management Decision*, 50(2), 189–206.

Gardner, H. (1985). *The Mind's New Science: A History of the Cognitive Revolution*. New York: Basic Books.

Gardner, L., & Stough, C. (2002). Examining the relationship between leadership and emotional intelligence in senior level managers. *Leadership & Organization Development Journal*, 23(2), 68–78.

Gasper, K., & Zawadzki, M. J. (2013). Want information? How mood and performance perceptions alter the perceived value of information and influence information-seeking behaviors. *Motivation and Emotion*, 37(2), 308–322.

Gintis, H., Smith, E. A., & Bowles, S. (2001). Costly signaling and cooperation. *Journal of Theoretical Biology*, 213(1), 103–119.

Goleman, D. P. (1995). *Emotional Intelligence: Why It Can Matter More Than IQ for Character, Health and Lifelong Achievement*. New York: Bantam Books.

Goleman, D. (2001). An EI-based theory of performance. In C. Cherniss & D. Goleman (Eds), *The Emotionally Intelligent Workplace: How to Select for, Measure, and Improve Emotional Intelligence in Individuals, Groups, and Organizations* (Vol. 1, pp. 27–44). San Francisco, CA: Jossey-Bass.

Hall, R. H., Clark, J. P., Giordano, P. C., Johnson, P. V., & van Roekel, M. (1977). Patterns of interorganizational relationships. *Administrative Science Quarterly*, 457–474.

Hambrick, D. C., & Mason, P. A. (1984). Upper echelons: The organization as a reflection of its top managers. *Academy of Management Review*, 9(2), 193–206.

Hardy, C., & Phillips, N. (1998). Strategies of engagement: Lessons from the critical examination of collaboration and conflict in an interorganizational domain. *Organization Science*, 9(2), 217–230.

Hawkes, K., & Bliege-Bird, R. (2002). Showing off, handicap signaling, and the evolution of men's work. *Evolutionary Anthropology: Issues, News, and Reviews: Issues, News, and Reviews*, 11(2), 58–67.

Higgins, C. A., & Judge, T. A. (2004). The effect of applicant influence tactics on recruiter perceptions of fit and hiring recommendations: A field study. *Journal of Applied Psychology*, 89(4), 622.

Hillman, A. J., Withers, M. C., & Collins, B. J. (2009). Resource dependence theory: A review. *Journal of Management*, 35(6), 1404–1427.

112   Strategic Interactions

Hirschhorn, L. (1990). Leaders and followers in a postindustrial age. *Journal of Applied Behavioral Science*, 26, 529–542.

Hodgkinson, G. P., & Healey, M. P. (2008). Cognition in organizations. *Annual Review of Psychology*, 59, 387–417.

Hodgkinson, G. P., & Johnson, G. (1994). Exploring the mental models of competitive strategists: The case for a processual approach. *Journal of Management Studies*, 31(4), 525–552.

Hoe, S. L. (2007). Is interpersonal trust a necessary condition for organisational learning? *Journal of Organisational Transformation & Social Change*, 4(2), 149–156.

Holloway, D. A., & van Rhyn, D. (2005). Effective corporate governance reform and organisational pluralism: Reframing culture, leadership and followership. In Lehman, C. R. (Ed.), *Corporate Governance: Does Any Size Fit? Advances in Public Interest Accounting*, 11, (pp. 303–328), Oxford: Elsevier.

Holmstrom, B. (1982). Moral hazard in teams. *The Bell Journal of Economics*, 324–340.

Howell, J., & Mendez, M. (2008). Three perspectives on followership. In Riggio, R., Chaleff, I., & Lipman-Blumen, J. (Eds.), *The Art of Followership: How Great Followers Create Great Leaders and Organizations* (pp. 25–40). San Francisco: Jossey-Bass.

Janney, J. J., & Folta, T. B. (2006). Moderating effects of investor experience on the signaling value of private equity placements. *Journal of Business Venturing*, 21(1), 27–44.

Jensen, M. C., & Meckling, W. H. (1976). Theory of the firm: Managerial behavior, agency costs and ownership structure. *Journal of Financial Economics*, 3(4), 305–360.

Johnson-Laird, P. N. (1983). *Mental Models: Towards a Cognitive Science of Language, Inference and Consciousness*. Cambridge: Cambridge University Press.

Johnston, V. (2003). The origin and function of pleasure. *Cognition and Emotion*, 17(2), 167–179.

Jones, C., Hesterly, W. S., & Borgatti, S. P. (1997). A general theory of network governance: Exchange conditions and social mechanisms. *Academy of Management Review*, 22(4), 911–945.

Kacmar, K. M., & Baron, R. A. (1999). Organizational politics: The state of the field, links to related processes, and an agenda for future research. In Ferris, G. R. (Ed.), *Research in Personnel and Human Resources Management* (Vol. 17, pp. 1–39). Stamford, CT: JAI Press.

Kahn, W. A., & Kram, K. E. (1994). Authority at work: Internal models and their organizational consequences. *Academy of Management Review*, 19(1), 17–50.

Kale, S. H. (1986). Dealer perceptions of manufacturer power and influence strategies in a developing country. *Journal of Marketing Research*, 387–393.

Kale, S. H. (1989). Dealer dependence and influence strategies in a manufacturer-dealer dyad. *Journal of Applied Psychology*, 74(3), 379.

Kaufmann, P. J., & Stern, L. W. (1988). Relational exchange norms, perceptions of unfairness, and retained hostility in commercial litigation. *Journal of Conflict Resolution*, 32(3), 534–552.

Kellerman, B. (2004). *Bad Leadership: What It Is, How It Happens, Why It Matters*. Boston: Harvard Business School Press.

Strategic Interactions   113

Kellerman, B. (2008). *Followership: How Followers Are Creating Change and Changing Leaders*. Boston: Harvard Business School Press.

Kellerman, B. (2012). *The End of Leadership*. New York, NY: Harper Business.

Kenny, D. A., & La Voie, L. (1984). The social relations model. *Advances in Experimental Social Psychology*, 18, 142–182.

Kernis, M. H., & Goldman, B. M. (2006). A multicomponent conceptualization of authenticity: Theory and research. *Advances in Experimental Social Psychology*, 38, 283–357.

Kipnis, D., & Schmidt, S. M. (1988). Upward-influence styles: Relationship with performance evaluations, salary, and stress. *Administrative Science Quarterly*, 528–542.

Kipnis, D., Schmidt, S. M., & Wilkinson, I. (1980). Intraorganizational influence tactics: Explorations in getting one's way. *Journal of Applied Psychology*, 65(4), 440.

Koeszegi, S. T. (2004). Trust-building strategies in inter-organizational negotiations. *Journal of Managerial Psychology*, 19(6), 640–660.

Kowalkowski, C., Witell, L., & Gustafsson, A. (2013). Any way goes: Identifying value constellations for service infusion in SMEs. *Industrial Marketing Management*, 42(1), 18–30.

Kumar, K., & Beyerlein, M. (1991). Construction and validation of an instrument for measuring ingratiatory behaviors in organizational settings. *Journal of Applied Psychology*, 76(5), 603–619.

Laing, A. W., & Lian, P. C. (2005). Inter-organisational relationships in professional services: Towards a typology of service relationships. *Journal of Services Marketing*, 19(2), 114–128.

Lazarus, S., & Folkman, S. (1984). *Stress, Coping and Adaptation*. New York: Springer.

Lazear, E. P. (1989). Pay equality and industrial politics. *Journal of Political Economy*, 97(3), 561–580.

Lazear, E. P., & Rosen, S. (1981). Rank-order tournaments as optimum labor contracts. *Journal of Political Economy*, 89(5), 841–864.

LeDoux, J. E. (2000). Emotion circuits in the brain. *Annual Review of Neuroscience*, 23(1), 155–184.

Leifer, R., & Mills, P. K. (1996). An information processing approach for deciding upon control strategies and reducing control loss in emerging organizations. *Journal of Management*, 22(1), 113–137.

Leslie, L. M., & Gelfand, M. J. (2012). The cultural psychology of social influence: Implications for organizational politics. In G. R. Ferris & D. C. Treadway (Eds.), *Politics in Organizations: Theory and Research Considerations*, (pp. 411–447). New York: Routledge, Taylor and Francis Group.

Lester, R. H., Certo, S. T., Dalton, C. M., Dalton, D. R., & Cannella Jr, A. A. (2006). Initial public offering investor valuations: An examination of top management team prestige and environmental uncertainty. *Journal of Small Business Management*, 44(1), 1–26.

Liu, K., Sun, L., Dix, A., & Narasipuram, M. (2001). Norm-based agency for designing collaborative information systems. *Information Systems Journal*, 11(3), 229–247.

Lubit, R. (2004). The tyranny of toxic managers: Applying emotional intelligence to deal with difficult personalities. *Ivey Business Journal*, 68(4), 1–7.

114 *Strategic Interactions*

Luthans, F., Luthans, K. W., & Luthans, B. C. (2004). Positive Psychological Capital: Beyond Human and Social Capital (p. 145). Management Department Faculty Publications (*Business Horizons*, 47(1), 45–50).

Luthans, F., Youssef, C. M., & Avolio, B. J. (2007). *Psychological capital: Developing the human competitive edge* (Vol. 198). Oxford: Oxford University Press.

Lyles, M. A., & Schwenk, C. R. (1992). Top management, strategy and organizational knowledge structures. *Journal of Management Studies*, 29(2), 155–174.

Macneil, I. R. (1980a). Economic analysis of contractual relations: Its shortfalls and the need for a rich classificatory apparatus. *Northwestern University Law Review*, 75, 10–18.

Macneil, I. R. (1980b). Power, contract, and the economic model. *Journal of Economic Issues*, 14(4), 909–923.

Mansbridge, J. (1999). Altruistic trust. In Warren, Mark (Ed.), *Democracy and Trust* (p. 290). New York: Cambridge University Press.

Mathieu, J. E., Heffner, T. S., Goodwin, G. F., Salas, E., & Cannon-Bowers, J. A. (2000). The influence of shared mental models on team process and performance. *Journal of Applied Psychology*, 85(2), 273.

Miller, T., & del Carmen Triana, M. (2009). Demographic diversity in the boardroom: Mediators of the board diversity–firm performance relationship. *Journal of Management Studies*, 46(5), 755–786.

Mintzberg, H. (1983) *Power in and Around Organizations*. Englewood Cliffs, NJ: Prentice-Hall.

Mintzberg, H. (1985). The organization as political arena. *Journal of Management Studies*, 22(2), 133–154.

Mintzberg, H., Ahlstrand, B. W., & Lampel, J. (1998). *Strategy Safari: The Complete Guide Through the Wilds of Strategic Management*. Harlow, UK: Financial Times, Prentice Hall.

Mintzberg, H., Raisinghani, D., & Theoret, A. (1976). The structure of "unstructured" decision processes. *Administrative Science Quarterly*, 246–275.

Miron-Spektor, E., Gino, F., & Argote, L. (2011). Paradoxical frames and creative sparks: Enhancing individual creativity through conflict and integration. *Organizational Behavior and Human Decision Processes*, 116(2), 229–240.

Möllering, G. (2003). A typology of supplier relations: From determinism to pluralism in inter-firm empirical research. *Journal of Purchasing and Supply Management*, 9(1), 31–41.

Moro, A., Fink, M., & Maresch, D. (2015). Reduction in information asymmetry and credit access for small and medium-sized enterprises. *Journal of Financial Research*, 38(1), 121–143.

Nonaka, I., & Takeuchi, H. (1995). *The Knowledge Creation Company: How Japanese Companies Create the Dynamics of Innovation*. New York: Oxford University Press.

Oliver, C. (1991). Strategic responses to institutional processes. *Academy of Management Review*, 16(1), 145–179.

Ortony, A., & Clore, G. L. (1989). Emotions, moods, and conscious awareness; comment on Johnson-Laird and Oatley's "the language of emotions: An analysis of a semantic field". *Cognition and Emotion*, 3(2), 125–137.

Parasuraman, A., Zeithaml, V. A., & Berry, L. L. (1988). Servqual: A multiple-item scale for measuring consumer perc. *Journal of Retailing*, 64(1), 12.

Penrose, E. T. (1959). *The Theory of the Growth of the Firm*. New York: Sharpe.

Strategic Interactions 115

Pfeffer, J. (1992). *Managing with Power: Politics and Influence in Organizations.* Boston: Harvard Business School Press.

Pfeffer, J. (1981). Management as symbolic action: The creation and maintenance of organizational paradigms. In Cummings, L. L. & Staw, B. M. (Eds.), *Research in Organizational Behavior* (vol. 13, pp. 1–52). Greenwich, CT: JAI Press.

Pfeffer, J., & Salancik, G. R. (1978). *The External Control of Organizations: A Resource Dependence Approach.* New York: Harper and Row Publishers.

Price, M. E., & van Vugt, M. (2014). The evolution of leader–follower reciprocity: The theory of service-for-prestige. *Frontiers in Human Neuroscience*, 8, 363.

Raes, A. M., Heijltjes, M. G., Glunk, U., & Roe, R. A. (2011). *The interface of the top management team and middle managers: A process model.* Academy of Management Review, 36(1), 102–126.

Redmond, M. V. (1989). The functions of empathy (decentering) in human relations. *Human Relations*, 42(7), 593–605.

Rosen, S. (1986). The theory of equalizing differences. In Ashenfelter, O. & Layard, R. (Eds.), *Handbook of Labor Economics* (pp. 641–692). Amsterdam: North Holland.

Rost, J. 2008. Followership: An outmoded concept. In Riggio, R. E., Chaleff, I., & Lipman-Blumen, J. (Eds.), *The Art of Followership: How Great Followers Create Great Leaders and Organizations.* San Francisco, CA: Jossey-Bass.

Rothschild, M., & Stiglitz, J. (1978). Equilibrium in competitive insurance markets: An essay on the economics of imperfect information. In *Uncertainty in Economics* (pp. 257–280).

Rothschild, M., & Stiglitz, J. E. (1976). Equilibrium in competitive insurance markets: An essay on the economics of imperfect information. *Quarterly Journal of Economics*, 90, 630–649.

Rouse, W. B., & Morris, N. M. (1986). On looking into the black box: Prospects and limits in the search for mental models. *Psychological Bulletin*, 100(3), 349.

Ruby, P., & Decety, J. (2004). How would you feel versus how do you think she would feel? A neuroimaging study of perspective-taking with social emotions. *Journal of Cognitive Neuroscience*, 16(6), 988–999.

Sabel, C. F. (1993). Studied trust: Building new forms of cooperation in a volatile economy. *Human Relations*, 46(9), 1133–1170.

Schmidt, S. M., & Kochan, T. A. (1977). Interorganizational relationships: Patterns and motivations. *Administrative Science Quarterly*, 220–234.

Schutte, N. S., Malouff, J. M., Bobik, C., Coston, T. D., Greeson, C., Jedlicka, C., . . . & Wendorf, G. (2001). Emotional intelligence and interpersonal relations. *The Journal of Social Psychology*, 141(4), 523–536.

Schwartz, N. (2012) Why researchers should think 'real-time': A cognitive rationale. In: Mehl M and Conner T (Eds), *Handbook of Research Methods forStudying Daily Life* (pp. 22–42). New York: Guildford Press.

Schwarz, N., & Clore, G. L. (2007). Feelings and phenomenal experiences. In Kruglanski, A. & Higgins, E. T. (Eds.), *Social Psychology: Handbook of Basic Principles* (2nd ed., pp. 385–400). New York, NY: Guilford.

Senge, P. M. (1990). *The Fifth Discipline: The Art and Practice of the Learning Organization.* New York: Doubleday.

Seligman, A. B. (1997). *The Problem of Trust.* Princeton: Princeton University Press.

Sharapov, D., & Ross, J. M. (2015). Whom should a leader imitate in multiple competitor settings? A contingency perspective. In *Academy of Management*

116 *Strategic Interactions*

Proceedings (Vol. 2015, No. 1, p. 18068). Briarcliff Manor, NY 10510: Academy of Management.

Snyder, C., Irving, L. M., & Anderson, S. A. (1991). Hope and health: Measuring the will and the ways. In Snyder, C. R. & Forsyth, D. R. (Eds.), *Handbook of Social and Clinical Psychology: The Health Perspective* (pp. 285–305). Elmsford, NY: Pergamon.

Spence, M. (2002). Signaling in retrospect and the informational structure of markets. *American Economic Review*, 92(3), 434–459.

Spence, M. (1973). Job market signaling. *The Quarterly Journal of Economics*, 87(3), 355–374.

Spence, M. (1976a). Informational aspects of market structure: An introduction. *The Quarterly Journal of Economics*, 591–597.

Spence, M. (1976b). Product differentiation and welfare. *The American Economic Review*, 66(2), 407–414.

Strauss, K., Griffin, M. A., & Rafferty, A. E. (2009). Proactivity directed toward the team and organization: The role of leadership, commitment and role-breadth self-efficacy. *British Journal of Management*, 20(3), 279–291.

Suazo, M. M., Martínez, P. G., & Sandoval, R. (2009). Creating psychological and legal contracts through human resource practices: A signaling theory perspective. *Human Resource Management Review*, 19(2), 154–166.

Tangpong, C., Michalisin, M. D., Traub, R. D., & Melcher, A. J. (2015). A review of buyer-supplier relationship typologies: Progress, problems, and future directions. *Journal of Business & Industrial Marketing*, 30(2), 153–170.

Tong, S. T., Van Der Heide, B., Langwell, L., & Walther, J. B. (2008). Too much of a good thing? The relationship between number of friends and interpersonal impressions on Facebook. *Journal of Computer-Mediated Communication*, 13(3), 531–549.

Uhl-Bien, M. Riggio, RE., Lowe, K.B. Carsten, M. (2014) Followership theory: A review and research agenda. *The Leadership Quarterly*, 25(1), 83–104.

Uslaner, E. M. (2002). *The Moral Foundations of Trust*. Cambridge University Press.

Van Kleef, G. A., De Dreu, C. K., & Manstead, A. S. (2006). Supplication and appeasement in conflict and negotiation: The interpersonal effects of disappointment, worry, guilt, and regret. *Journal of Personality and Social Psychology*, 91(1), 124.

Venkatesh, R., Kohli, A. K., & Zaltman, G. (1995). Influence strategies in buying centers. *The Journal of Marketing*, 71–82.

Vogt, B. A. (2005). Pain and emotion interactions in subregions of the cingulate gyrus. *Nature Reviews Neuroscience*, 6(7), 533.

Walsh, J. P. (1995). Managerial and organizational cognition: Notes from a trip down memory lane. *Organization Science*, 6(3), 280–321.

Williamson, O. E. (1985). *The Economic Institutions of Capitalism: Firms, Markets, Relational Contracting*. New York: Free Press.

Williamson, O. E. (1975). *Markets and Hierarchies: Analysis and Antitrust Implications*. New York: Free Press.

Witt, L. A., Andrews, M. C., & Kacmar, K. M. (2000). The role of participation in decision-making in the organizational politics-job satisfaction relationship. *Human Relations*, 53(3), 341–358.

Yamagishi, T., & Yamagishi, M. (1994). Trust and commitment in the United States and Japan. *Motivation and Emotion*, 18(2), 129–166.

Yammarino, F. J., Spangler, W. D., & Bass, B. M. (1993). Transformational leadership and performance: A longitudinal investigation. *Leadership Quarterly*, 4, 81–102.

Yerkes, R. M., & Dodson, J. D. (1908). The relation of strength of stimulus to rapidity of habit-formation. *Journal of Comparative Neurology and Psychology*, 18(5), 459–482.

Yulk, G. A. (1998). *Leadership in Organizations*. Englewood Cliffs, NJ: Prentice-Hall.

Yukl, G. A. (1989). Managerial leadership: A review of theory and research. *Journal of Management*, 15(2), 251–289.

Zajonc, R. B. (1980). Feeling and thinking: Preferences need no inferences. *American Psychologist*, 35(2), 151.

Zeidner, M., Matthews, G., & Roberts, R. D. (2004). Emotional intelligence in the workplace: A critical review. *Applied Psychology*, 53(3), 371–399.

Zhang, Y., & Wiersema, M. F. (2009). Stock market reaction to CEO certification: The signaling role of CEO background. *Strategic Management Journal*, 30(7), 693–710.

Zoogah, D. B. (Ed.), (2014). *Advancing Research Methodology in the African Context: Techniques, Methods, and Designs*. Bingley, UK: Emerald. https://doi.org/10.1108/S1479-8387201410.

6 Strategic Outcomes

What outcomes do strategic followership yield? Strategic followership is valuable because of the outcomes it creates. In this chapter, I discuss theories that deal with strategic outcomes. Specifically, I focus on theoretical perspectives that center on strategic value. I also discuss the levels of strategic followership because of the increasing centralization of levels theory in management and the convergence of the micro-foundation with the macro-foundations perspectives. I begin with strategic value analysis followed by strategic outcomes, and levels of analysis.

6.1 Strategic Value

In the Introduction to this book I advanced some assumptions of strategic followership, two of which are equality and readiness. Using those assumptions, I elaborate on the strategic value curve. I mentioned in that chapter that "the resultant value curve is concave for restorative value but convex for transcendent value such that followers will weight restorative action more than transcendent action (Vr > Vt)." In their theory of business, Donaldson and Walsh (2015) discuss the concept of value. They note that the term *value* is common in discussions of economics and business but is "often left undefined, or when defined, interpreted through a price mechanism or systematized preference rankings (including the analysis of indifference)" (p. 189). They identify typologies of value, the first of which is positive versus negative. While positive value refers to "a reason for acting when the object of the act is seen as worthy of pursuit," negative value constitutes "a reason for not acting or avoiding something undesirable or aversive" (p. 189). This distinction is important because strategic followership centers on positive value (Zoogah, 2014). A strategic follower deems uplifting the leader, relationship, department, organization, etc.) as worthy of pursuit. He or she would not act in a way that negatively affects the constituent. That motive serves as the follower's reason for acting restoratively or transcendently. In that case, value might be viewed as a matter of personal taste (i.e., personal agency).

The second typology is intrinsic versus nonintrinsic. This distinction is not based specifically on agency. Intrinsic value refers to the worth of an object, action, or person. It is a higher order reason. As Donaldson and Walsh (2015) indicated, "when something that is 'worthy of pursuit' does not have its own value derived from a higher-order value, it counts as an Intrinsic Value." They define "an intrinsic value as a form of value whose worth does not depend on its ability to achieve other positive values" (p. 190). It is a final reason for acting. Intrinsic values, in turn, possess an 'objective' normative status. When something lacks this internal worth, it has non-intrinsic value. In other words, its value is for something else. It is derivative. Related to strategic followership intrinsic and non-intrinsic values are applicable. While intrinsic value centers on transcendent followership, nonintrinsic value centers on restorative followership. Restorative followers behave restoratively because the relational constituent is negatively affected while transcendent followers, who could do without extraordinary behaviors, do so for the intrinsic value.

The third typology is individual versus collective. They refer to collective value as the agglomeration of the business constituents' benefits, net of any harmful business outcomes. That is because of their interest in advancing the theory of business. Given my interest in followership, collective value refers to the benefits accrued to relational constituents, beyond those accruing to the follower, from a follower's restorative and transcendent actions. The summation of restorative and transcendent values, in one sense, constitutes collective value (i.e., strategic value). This is likely when the follower relates with both a bad leader, on one hand, where he or she has to generate restorative value, and a good leader, on the other hand, where transcendent value is generated. This might center on only one constituent (e.g., leader). In another sense, collective value is the summation of either restorative value over several instances that pertain to multiple constituents. Admittedly, I recognize that "the satisfaction of a set of values for an individual person, not to mention a group of people, is impossible to measure accurately on a simple numerical continuum" (Donaldson & Walsh, 2015: 191) because of the problem of incommensurability. Nevertheless, I agree with Donaldson and Walsh that collective value as "an agglomeration of benefits, not an aggregation of benefits," seems better.

In sum, strategic value of followership takes into consideration positive, intrinsic, and collective forms because followership is an exchange and transactive. However, given that exchange and transactive terms have negative or aversive components from a strategic standpoint (undermining or harming a competitor so as to gain the upper hand), it is the positive aspects of exchange and transaction that should be considered consistent with strategic followership which is positively valenced (Zoogah, 2014). Analysis of strategic value can thus only be considered exchange value

120   *Strategic Outcomes*

analysis or transactive value analysis to the extent that the focus is solely on the positive elements. That is important when a follower engage in relational or transactive exchange with leaders. The latter may be good (but suboptimal) or bad. The strategic value curve (SVC) can therefore be analyzed based on the equality paradigm (EP) and the willingness (a specific form of motivation) of a follower to contribute value (WC), as well as the competence of that actor (a specific form of ability) to contribute value (CC) and the opportunity (a specific form of environmental beneficence) to contribute value, (OC). SVC can be expressed as follows:

$$SVC = \text{restorative value} (RV) + \text{maintenance value} (MV) + \text{transcendent value} (TV);$$
$$\text{and, } TV > MV > RV.$$
$$RV = f(WC \times OC) + CC]$$
$$MV = f(WC + CC) \times OC]$$
$$TV = f(WC \times OC \times CC]$$

Thus,

$$\text{If EP} >= 1, \text{ then SVC} = \max(WC \times CC \times OC) = TV$$
$$\text{If EP} = 0, \text{ then SVC} = 0 = \min(WC \times CC \times OC) = MV$$
$$\text{IF EP} < 0, \text{ then} = \min(WC \times CC \times OC) > SVC < \max(WC \times CC \times OC)$$

Restorative value is expressed as such because of the follower's courage, which is stronger. Searching for an opportunity may not be needed. Similarly, maintenance value is expressed that way because of the obligation derived from the role demand as stipulated in the job description. There is no need for the follower to wait for an opportunity. Last, transcendent value is expressed as such mainly because of the challenge of overcoming a hurdle (Bateman & Porath, 2003), which is required in transcendent behavior.

The strategic value expressed in the preceding equations assumes that the follower is capable. When we account for the capability of the follower, then the optimal value generation capability of the follower is expressed in the following equation:

$$OVGC = f\left[\text{sx.m.a.}(-q)\right],$$

where

> OVGC = optimal value generation capability,
> sx = situational complexity,
> m = degree of motivation,
> a = ability to generate value, and
> −q = dysfunctional traits.

6.2 Strategic Outcomes

Strategic followership yields strategic outcomes (Zoogah, 2014). It is therefore important to understand that strategy goes hand in hand with processes, resources (positions), and capabilities. Rumelt (2011: 6) defines a strategy is "a coherent set of analyses, concepts, policies, arguments, and actions that respond to a high-stakes challenge." A good strategy therefore has a kernel comprising (1) prescient diagnoses, (2) a guiding policy, and (3) coherent action (Rumelt, 2011). This kernel centers on the strategic outcomes. A review of the literature shows a number of strategic outcomes, the first of which is organizational effectiveness. There is consensus among management scholars that organizational effectiveness, of which performance is an indicator, is multidimensional and is manifested in various perspectives (Cameron & Whetten, 1983). I focus on four outcomes believed to be of greater significance in this economic epoch but also consistent with strategic followership: productivity, innovation, learning, and advantages. Basically, productivity is a state of affairs that exists when the outcomes achieved from the organization's valuable output of products or services are greater than the costs associated with the inputs needed to yield the desired state of affairs (Cronin & Gudim, 1986: 95). It is a function of efficiency and effectiveness. Efficiency is determined as the costs of inputs into an organization's production system compiled against the value of the outputs. If the latter is greater, the entity is operating efficiently. Effectiveness, on the other hand, is concerned with the quality and utility of output and is arguably assessed by the organizations' stakeholders, including customers, employees, executives, suppliers, financiers, and shareholders (Flowerdew & Whitehead, 1974). Flowerdew and Whitehead (1974) for example, view effectiveness as a composite index of valuable outputs that should include all beneficial effects of the project being assessed.

Research in interfirm (Oliver, 1990) and buyer–supplier (Terpend, Tyler, Krause, & Handfield, 2008) relationships suggest that firms, as followers, often gain productivity. It is therefore likely that followers, particularly firms may interact with leaders to maximize productivity. In the NUMMI joint venture, General Motors sought to learn the productivity system of Toyota, albeit with little success (Gomes-Casseres, 2009). Nonetheless, it is probable that follower may maximize its efficiency and effectiveness through its relationship with a leader. It may adapt or adopt the productivity practices of the leader with great success (Zoogah, 2014). Innovation, defined as "the development and implementation of new ideas by people who over time engage in transactions with others within an institutional order" (Van de Ven, 1986), is not confined only to the new technology of products. Turnarounds, mergers, restructuring, total quality, continuous improvement programs, globalization projects,

122 Strategic Outcomes

and several others that are also the forefront of many transformations require organizational capacity to translate ideas or intentions into new action. One way that transformation takes place is through the interactive process among people about new ideas in, as well as across, organizational contexts (Bouwen & Fry, 1991). The organizational innovation process focuses on the ways people become organized around new tasks and the consequences of these efforts on further organizational functioning after the implementation of the innovation. Strategic followership proposes that followers contribute value to their organizations in both bad and good leadership contexts. To the extent that a leader is behaving badly (i.e., incompetently or unethically), as follower in an exchange relationship may engage in restorative or transcendent actions that yield innovative ideas. Followers, as individuals or organizations, can thus influence innovation (Bouwen & Fry, 1988).

Organizational learning, defined as the increased process capacity to innovate in the future within that same organizational setting (Argyris & Schon, 1978), occurs organically and vicariously. A firm as follower can learn from another one in a leading role. In their study of Korean firms in the semiconductor industry, Mathews and Cho (2001) observed that latecomer firms are not "late entrants"; rather, the latecomer firm's market entry is a "matter of strategic choice" because the latecomer firms "are very well established and well-endowed firms which delay entry until technological and market trends are clear—and then move in with superior forces to take the lion's share of the market." They contend that it is a rational "followership" strategy, a matter of strategic choice. The buyer–supplier literature also suggests that suppliers sometimes learn the processes of buyer firms for imitative purposes or because of strategic coercion (Heide & John, 1990; Han, Wilson, & Dant, 1993). Single-loop (when a following firm improves its product in the first generation) and double-loop learning (when improvements in "combinative capabilities" of initial yields lead to improvements with each generation of the product) can occur as following firms' operations move from development to mass production (Mathews & Cho, 2001; Ross & Sharapov, 2015).

Firms form relationships to achieve strategic outcomes, one of which is competitive advantage. Zaheer and Venkatraman (1994) define competitive advantage as "the advantage to the firm differentiating at the level of the network used to develop a business relationship" (p. 186). However, it is suggested that just as organizations can gain an advantage by competing with others, they can also gain an advantage by cooperating. This is because the introduction of cooperative ventures to the strategy literature resulted in a "cooperative advantage" perspective because competitive advantage is viewed as insufficient for optimizing outcomes (Lei, Slocum, & Pitts, 1997; Skrabec, 1999; Zoogah, 2012). Studies show that collaboration yields more gains for the actors—resource acquisition,

Strategic Outcomes 123

profitability, market share, innovation, and other outcomes that contribute to organizational effectiveness—in the endeavor than does competition (see Shenkar & Reuer, 2006; Zaheer & Venkatraman, 1994). Building on Zaheer and Venkatraman's (1994) definition of cooperative advantage as "the advantage accruing to a set of firms joining in the creation of a common network" (p. 186), Zoogah (2012) defines cooperative advantage as the advantage that is associated with working in concert with others and developing capacities to connect individual efforts that harness resources and yield outcomes beyond what individual organizations could achieve. He suggests collaborative structure, governance, agency, and resources as sources by which firms can gain cooperative advantage consistent with the characteristics of his definition—mutual interdependence, collaboration, and shared outcomes and costs.

Competitive and cooperative advantages can be achieved through the strategic followership of firms and individuals. For the latter, it is through emergence processes (Kozlowski & Klein, 2000) in contrast to the former, which is through interactive processes. The collaborative structure that links a following firm to a leading firm may drive the two organizations to seek efficiency advantages to structure their collaborations differently from those that seek innovation advantages. In addition, the inability of a following firm and leading firm to predict the behavior of the partner can be reduced through economic and social mechanisms that minimize opportunism, the tendency of collaborative partners to act with guile (Williamson, 1985, 1991). Furthermore, agency controls, such as monitoring and incentives' alignment, optimize interactions and collaborative outcomes of a following and a leading firm, particularly if they have interdependent orientations. Transparency facilitates achievement of advantages from cooperation by minimizing the ability of one party to act in ways contrary to the collaborative partners' interests. Firms that are transparent not only neutralize opportunistic behavior but also attract other firms, thereby increasing the set of opportunities in the collaboration network. Last, resources that facilitate cooperative advantage include competencies, experience, and relationships of a following firm. Competencies (i.e., skills, knowledge, and abilities) are important not only for establishing, governing, and controlling but also for exploiting gains from relationships with other organizations (Ployhart, 2015). Indeed, other strategic outcomes—relational capital, legitimacy, order, competence, effectiveness—are suggested by the strategic theories I reviewed in the previous chapters.

One major issue of significance is the level of analysis of strategic followership vis-a-vis these strategic outcomes. Strategic followership is proposed as both emergent (individual behaviors that eventually influence organizational outcomes) and interactive (one organization's behaviors that affects another's outcomes). In that regard it is of interest to

124 *Strategic Outcomes*

organizational behavior and human resources management scholars who are interested in the strategic value of individual employees' behaviors (i.e., macro-foundation) and strategic management scholars who are interested in the behavior of employees and how they influence the outcomes of organizations (i.e., micro-foundations). While the former is emergent, the latter is contextual. Nonetheless, both involve a levels issue. For more than forty years now, micro-organizational scholars have been contemplating a shift from purely micro-individual-level research to meso- or multilevel research (House, Rousseau, & Thomas-Hunt, 1995). At the beginning of the century, levels theory became central (Kozlowski & Klein, 2000), a shift that was deemed laudable and essential (Kozlowski & Klein, 2000). Multilevel research is complex and rigorous to the extent that a researcher is able to capture much of the nested complexity in organizations. That complexity is increased when additional levels such as the dyadic relations between followers and leaders (Uhl-Bien, Riggio, Lowe, & Carsten, 2014).

Levels of analysis theory posit that the effects of cognitions, affect, and behaviors are truly observable at their appropriate level. Consequently, individual cognitions are likely to be observed meaningfully at the individual level. Collective levels from dyads or groups are also likely to be observed meaningfully at the dyad or group level. To the extent that the psychological or strategic characteristics traverse levels, then that crossing has to be taken into consideration. There are two ways strategic followership characteristics cross levels. First, individual behaviors could cross to dyadic, group, or organizational levels to influence outcomes therein. This is emergent (Kozlowski & Klein, 2000). Emergent level of analysis should appropriately be used to examine the emergence process if that is the interest. However, traditional approaches, albeit archaic now, such as aggregation, may be used to examine the outcomes that arise from the emergence process. Second, attributes of higher level units—organizations and groups—can also influence outcomes at the lower (i.e., individual) level. This is contextual (Kozlowski & Klein, 2000). How organizational characteristics such as structure and culture influence restorative and transcendent behavior of followers can be examined contextually. To the extent that an organization has a punitive culture (one that does not value subordinates challenging authority), then followers are unlikely to engage in restorative behaviors. Constructive culture may also influence strategic followers to engage in transcendent behaviors (Bateman & Porath, 2003).

Conclusion

In these chapters I reviewed theories that may be used for investigation of strategic followership, particularly at the firm level. Followership at the firm level is emergent and needs to be examined critically as a mechanism for the enhancement of competitive positioning. Competitive positioning refers to

Strategic Outcomes 125

the choice of a firm in securing its market (Hooley, Broderick, & Broderick, 1998). Porter (1996) identifies three ways in which firms position themselves in the market: *variety position* which centers on the product, *needs-based position* that focuses on the design of its product to meet the needs of a target constituency, and *access-based position* that is based on the accessibility of a chosen market segment. Competitive positioning essential focuses on how a company gains and sustains competitive advantage (Porter, 1996). Organizations use assets (resource-based view; Barney, 1991; Wernerfelt, 1984) and capabilities (Mahoney, 1995; Teece, Pisano, & Shuen, 1992) for competitive positioning (Hooley et al., 1998). The organizational perspective of strategic followership may contribute to the positioning.

Research shows that assets and capabilities include relationships. For example, the interorganizational relationships literature shows that organizations can position themselves using the sets of relationships they have (i.e., social capital) and capabilities (governance of those relationships) they possess. Consistent with Day's (1994) distinction of assets as resource endowments the organization has accumulated (e.g., social capital) and capabilities as the complex bundle of skills that binds the assets together and enables them to be deployed advantageously, I assert that strategic followership is assetizable to the extent that it can be deployed to achieve and sustain the market positioning of organizations. It becomes a capability when it manifests as a complex bundle of skill that facilitates superior coordination of functional activities. To the extent that organizations are able to harness strategic followership as a capability, they are likely to achieve superior outcomes relative to their competitors. That depends on the empirical evidence garnered from research using the micro- and macro-theoretical lenses suggested in this book.

References

Argyris, C., & Schon, D. (1978). *Organizational Learning: A Theory of Action Approach*. Reading, MA: Addison Wesley.

Barney, J. (1991). Firm resources and sustained competitive advantage. *Journal of Management*, 17(1), 99–120.

Bateman, T. S., & Porath, C. (2003). Transcendent behavior. In Cameron, K. S., Dutton, J. E., & Quinn, R. E. (Eds.), *Positive Organizational Scholarship: Foundations of a New Discipline* (pp. 122–137). San Francisco: Berrett-Koehler.

Bouwen, R., & Fry, R. (1988). An Agenda for managing organizational innovation and development in the 1990's. In Lambrecht, M. (Ed.), *Corporate Revival* (pp. 153–172). Leuven: University Press.

Bouwen, R., & Fry, R. (1991). Organizational innovation and learning: Four patterns of dialog between the dominant logic and the new logic. *International Studies of Management & Organization*, 21(4), 37–51.

Cameron, K. S., & Whetten, D. A. (1983) Organizational effectiveness: One model or several? In Cameron, K. S., & Whetten, D. A. (Eds.), *Organizational*

126 Strategic Outcomes

Effectiveness: A Comparison of Multiple Methods (pp. 1–24). New York: Academic Press.

Cronin, B., & Gudim, M. (1986). Information and productivity: A review of research. *International Journal of Information Management*, 6, (2), 85–101.

Day, G. S. (1994). The capabilities of market-driven organizations. *Journal of Marketing*, 58, 37–52.

Donaldson, T., & Walsh, J. P. (2015). Toward a theory of business. *Research in Organizational Behavior*, 35, 181–207.

Flowerdew, A. D. J., & Whitehead, C. M. E. (1974). *Cost-Effectiveness and Cost/Benefit Analysis in Information Science* (pp. 36–47) London: London School of Economics and Political Science (OSTI Report 5206).

Gomes-Casseres, B. 2009. *Nummi: What Toyota Learned and GM Didn't*. Harvard Business Publishing. Retrieved from https://hbr.org/2009/09/nummi-what-toyota-learned on June 23, 2018.

Han, S. L., Wilson, D. T., & Dant, S. P. (1993). Buyer-supplier relationships today. *Industrial Marketing Management*, 22(4), 331–338.

Heide, J. B., & John, G. (1990). Alliances in industrial purchasing: The determinants of joint action in buyer-supplier relationships. *Journal of Marketing Research*, 24–36.

Hooley, G., Broderick, A., & Möller, K. (1998). Competitive positioning and the resource-based view of the firm. *Journal of Strategic Marketing*, 6(2), 97–116.

House, R. J., Rousseau, D. M., & Thomas-Hunt, M. (1995). The third paradigm: Meso organizational research comes to age. *Research in Organizational Behavior*, 17, 71–114.

Kozlowski, S. W. J., & Klein, K. J. 2000. A multilevel approach to theory and research in organizations: Contextual, temporal, and emergent processes. In Klein, K. J. & Koslowski, S. W. J. (Eds.), *Multilevel Theory, Research, and Methods in Organizations* (pp. 3–90). San Francisco: Jossey Bass

Lei, D., Slocum Jr, J. W., & Pitts, R. A. (1997). Building cooperative advantage: Managing strategic alliances to promote organizational learning. *Journal of World Business*, 32(3), 203–223.

Mahoney, J. T. (1995). The management of resources and the resource of management. *Journal of Business Research*, 33, 91–10.

Mathews, J. A., & Cho, D. S. (2001). Combinative capabilities and organizational learning in latecomer firms: The case of the Korean semiconductor industry. *Journal of World Business*, 33(4), 139–156.

Oliver, C. (1990). Determinants of interorganizational relationships: Integration and future directions. *Academy of Management Review*, 15, 241–265.

Ployhart, R. E. (2015). Strategic organizational behavior (STROBE): The missing voice in the strategic human capital conversation. *Academy of Management Perspectives*, 29(3), 342–356.

Porter, M. (1996). What is strategy? *Harvard Business Review*, 74(6), 61–80.

Ross, J. M., & Sharapov, D. (2015). When the leader follows: Avoiding dethronement through imitation. *Academy of Management Journal*, 58(3), 658–679.

Rumelt, R. (2011). The perils of bad strategy. *McKinsey Quarterly*, 1(3).

Shenkar, O., & Reuer, J. J. (2006). The alliance puzzle: Known terrain, black boxes, and the road ahead. In Shenkar, O. & Reuer, J. J. (Eds.), *Handbook of Strategic Alliances* (pp. 3–14). London: Sage Publications.

Skrabec Jr, Q. R. (1999). Cooperative advantage—A new measure of performance. *National Productivity Review*, 18(2), 69–73.

Teece, D., Pisano, G., & Shuen, A. (1992). Dynamic capabilities and strategic management. CCC Working Paper No. 90-8, Haas School of Business, University of California at Berkeley.

Terpend, R., Tyler, B. B., Krause, D. R., & Handfield, R. B. (2008). Buyer—Supplier relationships: Derived value over two decades. *Journal of Supply Chain Management*, 44(2), 28–55.

Uhl-Bien, M., Riggio, R. E., Lowe, K. B., & Carsten, M. K. (2014). Followership theory: A review and research agenda. *The Leadership Quarterly*, 25(1), 83–104.

Van de Ven, A. H. (1986). Central problems in the management of innovation. *Management Science*, 32(5), 590–607.

Wernerfelt, B. (1984). A resource-based view of the firm. *Strategic Management Journal*, 5(2), 171–180.

Williamson, O. E. (1985). *The Economic Institutions of Capitalism*. New York: Free Press.

Williamson, O. E. (1991). Comparative economic organization: The analysis of discrete structural alternatives. *Administrative Science Quarterly*, 269–296.

Zaheer, A., & Venkatraman, N. (1994). Determinants of electronic integration in the insurance industry: An empirical test. *Management Science*, 40(5), 549–566.

Zoogah, D. (2014). *Strategic Followership: How Followers Impact Organizational Effectiveness*. Springer.

Zoogah, D. B. (2012). A cooperative advantage: An alternative informed by institutional theory. *Industrial and Organizational Psychology*, 5(1), 116–119.

Index

Page numbers in *italics* refer to figures and those in bold refer to tables.

action imitation 20
active participation **90**, 92
activity-passivity dimension 14
adaptation, defined 39
affect; *see also* strategic affect:
    defined 105; as information 106;
    psychological theories related to 20
affect-induced cognitive processing
    106
affective knowledge 106
affective states 105–106, 108
agency theory 6, **22**, 23, 94–95
alienated followers 14
alliance partners 53, 80
antiprototypes, follower 16
Art of War, The (Tzu) 18
asymmetric interactions **90**, 91–94;
    I 91–93; II 93–94
authenticity **90**, 93
authority-ranking relationships 60

behaviors: bad leadership 1, 2–3, 21,
    27, 29, 44, **47**, 60, 103, 106, 107,
    122; competence as driver of 3;
    cooperative 2, **90**; good leadership
    3, 21, 29, 44, 54, 60, 77, 106,
    107, 122; lock-out and lock-in
    80–81; psychological theories
    related 20; regulatory 50; strategic
    behavior theory 76–78
benign followers 14
best alternative to no agreement
    (BATNA) 82
bottom-up approach 3
boundary-spanner 80
brinkmanship, defined 82
bureaucracy 23
business policy perspective 20, 21

business strategy 18
buyer-supplier relationships 5, 52, 89,
    121, 122

capabilities theory 78
capability routines 48
capital theory, psychological
    100–101, 104–105
chaotic dynamics 52–53
coercive tactics 91, 94
cognition, defined 100
cognitive attributes 103–104
cognitive bias 67, 100
collaborative leadership, defined 88
collective value 119
companies, categories of 4
competence: behaviors driven by 3;
    in independent role orientation 15;
    in leverage 59; in resource-based
    theory 78; in social construction
    theory 56; in social exchange
    theory 108; in strategic interactions
    90, 93–94; in strategic outcomes
    123; in strategic problem 42–43;
    in strategic role contexts 21; in
    strategic value 120
competence theory 78, 103–104
competition 97–98
competitive advantage 4; in
    competence theory 103; in
    psychological capital theory 104;
    in relational dynamics theory 52;
    in resource-based theory 78; in
    strategic leverage 40; in strategic
    outcomes 122–123; in transcendent
    followership 23
competitive positioning 124–125
compulsive followers 14

Index 129

conditional dynamics 52–53
conformist followers 14
conformity 16, 76, 90, 94
connector 80
constructive strategy 77
consultation: defined 92–93; tactics 90, 92–93
contribution of followers 5, 28, 99; *see also* readiness
controlling tactics 77–78
Cooper, Cynthia 2, 3
cooperation: in game theory 43–44, 69; as influence tactic 89, 90, **90**
cooperative advantage 122–123
cooperative behaviors 2, 90
cooperative games 43–44
counterconformity 94
counterdependent orientation 89, 90, 91–94
crisis decision theory 70–71
culture: defined 23; within organizations 23–24; theory **22**, 46–47, 76

decision-making; *see also* strategic decisions: bureaucracy and 23; in competence theory 101; in consultation 92–93; in crisis decision theory 70–71; dynamic capabilities and 78; in game theory 43–46, 68–70; in negotiation theory 81; in prospect theory 7, 73–75; in social systems theory 58; in strategic cognition theory 101; in structuration theory 56
demand tactics 74, 77, **90**, 91
dependence, defined 90
dependent orientation 89, 90, 91–94
disturbance view 51–52
dominance-submission dimension 14
double-loop learning, defined 122
dynamic capabilities, defined 78–79

economic exchange theory 24–25, 95–96
efficacy 16, 28–29, 101, 103, 104–105
efficiency 76–77, 121, 123
emotion 82, 105–106, 108
emotional intelligence (EI) 107–108
empathy **90**, 93, 108
enactment 103
endorsement 3, 107
ends 18–19

Enron 2
entity perspective 51
environmental context 3, 19, 20, 59
equality; *see also* value creation: in game theory 70; in network theory 80; in strategic value curve 118, 120; in symmetric interactions 89–90
equality-matching 43, 59–60
equality paradigm (EP) 120
ESS theory 68
evolutionary economics 47–48, 78
evolutionary stable strategy (ESS) 68
exchange theory 8, **22**, 24–25, 95–96; economic 24–25, 95–96; social 8, 24, 107–108
exchange value analysis 119–120
exemplary followers 14

feeling 105–106, 108
flatness 5, 75
follower: antiprototypes 16; prototypes 15–16; role orientations 15; schema of, passive and proactive 15; styles of 14; of toxic leaders, categories of 14–15; types of 14–15
follower agency 57–58
follower-leader exchanges 3, 8, 48, 99, 105
followership; *see also* strategic followership: defined 13; as role 13–18
following firm 4–5; alliance partners as 53; resource-based theories and 78; restorative followership and 27; strategic interactions and 89, 90, **90**, 90–91; strategic leverage and 27, 40; strategic outcomes and 123; strategic problem and 43; strategic role context and 19, 59, 60; strategic vulnerability and 42; transcendent followership and 23
formal institutions 27

gains function 75
game theory 43–46, 68–70
General Motors 80
good leadership behaviors 3, 21, 29, 44, 54, 60, 77, 106, 107, 122
governance mechanisms 25

harmonizing/harmony 3, 18
Health Management Organizations (HMOs) 42

130 *Index*

hedging 3
hope 101, 104–105

imitation 3, 4, 20
implementer followership 14
implicit leadership theories (ILTs)
  15–16
impulsive followers 14
incentives, defined 82
incompetence 2, 16, 52
independent role orientation 15
individualist followership 14
individual value 119
influence, defined 88–89
influence dynamics 43, 59, 60, 89, 90,
  99–100
influence interface exchange 39
informal institutions 27
information asymmetry 7; defined
  24; overview of 21, **22**, 24; in
  restorative followership 28; in
  signaling theory 98, 99; in strategic
  decisions 72–73; in strategic
  interactions 89, 90; in transcendent
  followership 24
information control **90**, 94
information exchange 89, 90, **90**, 94
information processing theory
  101–102
ingratiation **90**
innovation 121–122
institutional theory 19, 20, **22**, 76, 94
institutions 50
insubordination 16, 17, 23
interactionism 30–31, 53
interactive perspective 21, 24, 50
interactive processes 122–123
interactive role orientation 15
interdependent orientation 89, **90**,
  91–94
interest-group paradox 31
internalized models of authority
  89–94, **90**
International Organization for
  Standardization (ISO) 19
interorganizational relationships 5,
  14, 20–21, 52, 60, 79
interpersonal strategic followership 4
intraorganizational relationships 20
intrinsic value 119

judgment 103

knowledge conversion, defined 106

latecomer firms 4–5, 26, 122
late entrants 4, 122
Lay, Kenneth 2
Leader-Member Exchange (LMX) 16,
  95
leaders, toxic 14–15
leader's entourage 14–15
leadership, defined 88
leading firm 4–5; alliance partners
  as 53; resource-based theories
  and 78; restorative followership
  and 27; strategic interactions
  and 89, 90, **90**; strategic leverage
  and 40; strategic outcomes and
  123; strategic problem and 43;
  strategic role context and 19, 59,
  60; strategic vulnerability and 42;
  transcendent followership and 23
learning, in strategic outcomes 122
legitimacy 3, 76–77, 98, 123
lock-out and lock-in behaviors 80–81
loss function 75

macro equivalent-economic exchange
  theory 95–96
macro-level research 1, 6–7, 9, **9**; in
  social exchange theory 95–96; in
  strategic actions 76; in strategic
  followership dynamics 50–51; in
  strategic outcomes 124; in strategic
  role context 20, 21
magnitude of transactions, defined 59
maintenance behaviors 3, 18
maintenance value 3, 18, 120
malevolent followers 15
management domain 6, 13, 15, 52
managerial cognition, defined 67
manipulative strategy 76–78
masochistic followers 14
means 18
mental models 7–8, 55, 100, 101,
  102–103
meso-level research 124
meso theoretical lenses 7
micro-level research 1, 6, 7, 9, **9**, 21;
  in information asymmetry 72; in
  relational dynamics theory 53; in
  social exchange theory 24, 95; in
  strategic followership dynamics
  50–51, 60; in strategic outcomes
  124; in strategic role context 20, 21
military strategy 18
mixed governance 25
modeling 60, 68, **90**, 93, 105

monitoring tactics 90, 92
mood 105–106
multilevel research 7, 20, 124
multinational corporations (MNCs) 58–59

naivety perspective 1
negative events, responding to 70
negative value 118
negotiation theory 81–82
network dynamics 53
networking 57
networks, defined 53
network theory 22, 79–81
New United Motor Manufacturing, Inc. (NUMMI) 80
nonconformity 71–72, 90, 94
noncooperative games 44
nonintrinsic value 119

optimal value generation capability (OVGC) 120
optimism 101, 104–105
organizational cognition, defined 67–68
organizational culture 23–24
organizational learning, defined 122
organizational politics 96
organizational routine theory 21, 22, 26, 47–48, 76
organizational symbolism 29, 49
outsourcing 25

partner followership 14
passive followers 14, 15
payoffs: in game theory 43–45, 46, 47, 69, 69; in restorative followership 28; in transcendent followership 25–26
performance theory 21, 22
periodic patterns of dynamics 52
pink noise patterns of dynamics 52
plea tactics 71–72
political science 15, 43
political theory 8, 22, 23, 31, 96, 100
positioning imitation 20
positive value 118
power, defined 42
power theory 22, 24
pragmatist followers 14
proactive follower 15
proactivity 90
productivity, defined 121
promises 90

prospect theory 7, 73–75
prototypes, follower 15–16
psychological capital, defined 104
psychological capital theory 100–101, 104–105
psychological frames 55
psychological perspectives of strategic followership 20, 72, 96
purity of intentions 5

readiness 5, 118; in signaling theory 98; in tournament theory 97
reference point 25, 73–75
reflection effect 75
relational contracting 24–25
relational dynamics theory 50, 51–54
relational leadership, defined 51
relational order 41
relational perspective 51
relationship, defined 53
relationship management, defined 108
resilience 101, 104–105
resource-based theory 7, 14, 21, 22, 42, 78–79, 125
resource dependence theory 7, 21, 22, 22–23, 76, 90, 91, 100
resource followership 14
restorative followership 22, 26–31
restorative value (RV) 6, 26–27, 30, 75, 99, 118–120
revolutionary perspective 1
role: cognitions based on 19–20; effectiveness 14; followership as 13–18; orientations 15
role theory, defined 13–14; see also strategic role theory
Ross, Jan-Michael 20
Rousseau, Jean-Jacques 69
routine, defined 48
routine theory 21, 22, 47–48, 76

screening, defined 72
self-awareness 108
self-efficacy 16, 104–105
self-management, defined 108
Sharapov, Dmitry 20
shifting-role orientation 15
SHOR (self-efficacy, hope, optimism, and resiliency) 104, 105
signaling, defined 72
signaling theory 8, 22; in restorative followership 28–29; in strategic interactions 98–99; in strategic trust 107

132 *Index*

single-loop learning, defined 122
social awareness, defined 108
social capital 57, 81, 92, 104, 125
social construction theory 50, 54–56
social exchange theory 8, 24, 107–108
social network theory 23, 79
social systems theory 50, 58
social value orientation (SVO) 8–9
spreads 26
stage dynamics 52
Stag Hunt game 69
stakeholder theory 21, **22**, 27, 100
stochastic dynamics 53
stratagem 18–19, 80, 95
strategic actions 7, 75–82; in negotiation theory 81–82; in network theory 79–81; overview 75–76; in resource-based theories 78–79; in strategic behavior theory 76–78; summary 83
strategic affect 105–108; *see also* affect; affect as information 106; in affective states 105–106, 108; defined 108; in social exchange theory 107–108; in strategic trust 107–108
strategic alliances 19, 52, 80, 89
strategic behavior theory 76–78
strategic choice, defined 71
strategic choice theory 71–72
strategic cognition 8, 100–105; in competence theory 103–104; in culture theory 47; in information processing theory 101–102; in psychological capital theory 100–101, 104–105; in relational dynamics theory 51, 52; in social construction theory 54; in strategic decisions 67–68; in strategic interactions 88; in strategic mental model theory 102–103
strategic cognition theory 8, 20, 101
strategic consensus, defined 67
strategic constraint 41
strategic context 39–43; differences in 58–60; overview 39–40; strategic constraint and 41; strategic interaction and 43, 60; strategic leverage and 40; strategic problem and 42–43; strategic vulnerability and 41–42
strategic context theories 58–60

strategic decisions 7, 67–75; in crisis decision theory 70–71; in game theory 68–70; in information asymmetry 72–73; overview 67–68; in prospect theory 73–75; in strategic choice theory 71–72; summary 83
strategic followership: background of 1–10; environment and process of 9, 9; strategic actions in 75–82; strategic affect in 105–108; strategic cognition in 100–105; strategic context in 39–43, 58–60; strategic decisions in 67–75; strategic interactions in 88–100; strategic outcomes in 121–124; strategic role in 13–32; strategic value in 118–120; theories of strategic situations in 43–50
strategic followership dynamics 50–58; relational dynamics theory 51–54; social construction theory 54–56; social systems theory 58; theories of strategic context and 58–60; theory of structuration 56–58
strategic interactions 7–8, 43, 60, 88–100; asymmetric interactions 90, 91–94; defined 89; game theory and 68; overview 88–89; strategic contexts and 43, 60; summary 99–100; symmetric interactions and 89, **90**, 90–91
strategic interaction theories 94–99; agency theory 94–95; exchange theory 95–96; political theory 96; signaling theory 98–99; tournament theory 97–98
strategic leadership 4–5, 76, 89, 95
strategic leverage 40
strategic management theories 6, 20, 32
strategic mental model theory 102–103
strategic objectives 3, 5, 8, 13; *see also* strategic role; in network theory 80; probability of achieving, calculating 39–40; in social exchange theory 108; strategic affect and 105; in strategic mental model theory 102; strategic problem and 43; in theory of structuration 57
strategic order 41

Index   133

strategic outcomes 121–124;
   advantages in, competitive and
   cooperative 122–123; innovation
   in 121–122; learning in 122; levels
   of analysis theory in 123–124;
   productivity in 121
strategic problem 42–43
strategic role 18–32; context
   19–21, **22**; defined 21; restorative
   followership and 26–31;
   transcendent followership and
   22–26
strategic role theory 6–7, 13–14, 16,
   19, 21, **22**, 31–32
strategic situations 7, 9, 9, 39–60; in
   strategic context 39–43, 58–60;
   in strategic followership dynamics
   50–58; in strategic role theory 21
strategic situations, theories of
   43–50; culture theory 46–47; game
   theory 43–46; institutions and
   50; organizational routine theory
   47–48; symbolism theory 48–49
strategic trust 7–8, 107–108
strategic value 8, 118–120; *see also*
   value; value creation; analysis of
   119–120; in competence theory
   104; in information asymmetry 24;
   in signaling theory 28; in symbolic
   capital 30–31; in tournament
   theory 26
strategic value curve (SVC) 6, 8, 98,
   118, 120
strategic vulnerability 41–42
strategy: defined 18–19, 121; ends
   in, identifying 18–19; means, to
   achieve ends 18
strategy formation 67, 100
structuration theory 50, 56–58
SVO (social value orientation) 8–9
symbolic interaction 30–31, 40
symbolism theory 8, **22**, 48–49
symmetric interactions 89, **90**, 90–91

threat tactics **90**, 91
top-down approach 20
tournament, defined 25, 97
tournament theory **22**, 25–26, 97–98
toxic leaders 14–15
Toyota 80

transactive value analysis 119–120
transcendent followership 3, **22**,
   22–26
transcendent value (TV) 6, 30–31,
   118–119, 120
trust building 92
Tzu, Sun 18

unethicality 2, 9, 17, 19, 28, 122

value 2–3; *see also* strategic value;
   value creation; competence
   to contribute 120; concept of
   118; curve 6, 8, 98, 118, 120;
   diminishing 2–3, 6, 56, 103;
   enhancement 6, 54, 74–75;
   function 74; individual *versus*
   collective 119; intrinsic *versus*
   nonintrinsic 119; maintenance 3,
   18, 120; opportunity to contribute
   120; optimal value generation
   capability 120; positive *versus*
   negative 118; restoration 6, 8, 28,
   67, 103; restorative 3, 6, 26–27,
   30, 75, 99, 103, 118–120; theory 8;
   transcendent 3, 6, 30–31, 118–119,
   120; willingness to contribute 120
value creation 3, 5, 6; *see also*
   equality; culture and 24; in game
   theory 46; in negotiation theory
   81; in relational dynamics theory
   52; in restorative followership
   28; in social systems theory 58; in
   strategic followership dynamics 50;
   in strategic mental model theory
   102, 103; in symbolism theory 49;
   in theory of structuration 57
vertical integration 25
vulnerability, defined 41–42

warnings **90**
War of the Sexes 70
Watkins, Sherron 2, 3
When The Leader Follows: Avoiding
   Dethronement Through Imitation
   (Ross and Sharapov) 20
withdrawn followers 14
WorldCom 2, 3

zone of normalcy 74–75